Understanding Collective Bargaining in Education

*Negotiations, Contracts and Disputes
Between Teachers and Boards*

by

Robert C. O'Reilly

The Scarecrow Press, Inc.
Metuchen, N.J. & London
1978

Library of Congress Cataloging in Publication Data

O'Reilly, Robert C., 1928-
    Understanding collective bargaining in education.

    Includes indexes.
    1. Collective bargaining--Local officials and
employees--United States. 2. Collective bargaining
--Teachers--United States. I. Title.
HD8005.6.U5073   331.89'041'3711   78-64495
ISBN 0-8108-1167-7

To

My wife,

Marjorie Ione O'Reilly

CONTENTS

v

LIST OF TABLES

MAPS AND FIGURES

PREFACE

This is a book on collective bargaining in the public employment sector. The primary focus is upon public schools but there is a substantial amount of material drawn from other public employment settings. As a result, inter-occupational comparisons can be made. In the past fifteen or twenty years, state after state has enacted statutes, authorizing bargaining within political subdivisions. Never having the endorsement of a federal statute which might bring new stability and uniformity to the field, public employees have, nonetheless, joined together for the purpose of addressing their employers. In some states, legislation has been comprehensive, with the lawmakers laying out in the statute the manner in which a local representative unit may come into existence, how it may achieve recognition, specifying negotiable items, and stipulating the methods by which impasse can be handled. Whatever particulars the law may have, it should be recognized by both parties to the bargaining that it constitutes a procedural constraint upon the traditions of public sector management, and the multitude of consequences of that phenomenon are largely unknown. Court litigation and arbitration cases are used to both complement and augment statutes.

Typically, state laws, when they are examined one by one, do less than indicated above. A law may be specific to a particular occupational category such as teachers, police, nurses, or fire fighters. Additionally, some laws may not clearly delineate how a local representative unit comes into being, or how impasse is resolved; or they may lack some other particularity which can be found in the public employee collective bargaining law of a neighboring state. It must be remembered, too, that about twelve states have no statutes about public sector bargaining, and where bargaining occurs in such states, it is only through local bilateral agreement.

In public employment, the industrial model does not perfectly apply, but it is helpful to a general or conceptual understanding of present-day worker attitudes and expectations. In a public hospital, for example, the nurses would comprise one segment of the total employee group and they would be labor; the trustees who are charged with the operation of the hospital, whether they are appointed or elected, would be management represented through their administrator. Admittedly, the application of the labor-management model to such an employment setting is fraught with problems. The industrial input-output concept is far too straightforward and simple to apply literally to a public hospital; the profit motive is absent. Other characteristics of difference could be listed, but a list of substantial length would not be a denial that much, if not all, of the growing public employment labor legislation has had its origins in earlier laws and cases directly related to private sector employment, and most of that since the Wagner Act of 1935.

Administrators of schools, cities, or counties will, in the bargaining setting, represent their governing board in some way. A hospital administrator may represent his trustees; a school superintendent may represent his board; a city manager may represent his city council; and so it goes, that in public settings professional administrators come to stand for the side of management. Like every rule, this one has exceptions, but they are few. Budget familiarity, policy implementation, and knowledge of cash flow are among the reasons which give credence to the representative model. There are many similarities in collective bargaining as it is carried on in any political subdivision.

On the side of labor, and partially because public bargaining is a new field, the local unit will typically seek representation from within its own group. Very large local units have turned to hiring their own professional representation. The vast majority of such public employee units are not large; the teacher's local in the New York City Public Schools, representing nearly 70,000 employees, is unique. Within the 700,000-member American Federation of State, County, and Municipal Employees (AFSCME), most locals would be small; the same would be true for locals of the National Education Association.

This is a book designed for both "sides" in the public employment sector. It is not a manual which will provide a bag of tricks for either administrators or employees. There is no intention to provide some position of advantage to one "side" over the other. Both administrators and employees will find--have found--their regional or national associations to be prolific publishers of how-to-do-it advisories. From personal research and observations of this rapidly developing labor arena, I believe that we have too much of how-to-do-it and too little of what-is-it. Understanding of contract negotiation and administration is the focus of this book.

The typical professional administrator now in office will not have had much exposure to, or interest in, the fields of economics and labor at the time he went through an academic development program. The employee selected by his peers as the leader would be unusual if he had substantial understanding of the American labor movement. This book is for both.

Membership data of the 1970s indicate a decline in the proportion of workers in unions--about one in four eligible workers is now a union member--which suggests that workers may lack information about union purposes and accomplishments that would persuade them into membership. In contrast to the general membership condition, one in every three eligible public employees is a member of a union. The National Education Association, with 1.9 million members, is now the second-largest labor organization in the United States, outranked only by the Teamsters. NEA membership grew by 400,000 between 1974 and 1976, though overall membership in American labor organizations declined by 767,000, or 3.8 per cent, in that same two-year period, as stated by the Bureau of Labor Statistics in a Labor Day, 1977 report. From 1974 through 1976, the American Federation of Teachers reported a membership increase from 444,000 to 446,000.

Although substantial union membership declines occurred in the private sector during the two years--largely in construction and manufacturing--union membership in the public sector increased during the same period. A 600,000 gain in state and local government employees offset a 100,000 drop in the number of federal employees who belong to labor organizations.

Increased knowledge about what can--and cannot--be done by the primary actors in the public bargaining sectors bodes well for the citizens represented by the boards, trustees and administrators, and the workers represented through their own colleagues. Out of ignorance, suspicion, and unrealistic expectations have come hostility, distrust, and bad contracts. The substance from which this book is composed derives from such fields as economics, management, labor history, statements of labor leaders, personal research of the author and actual agreements. Some reader familiarity with various public organizations is presumed.

A single book is going to have limited impact in such a vast field. The ideas, concepts, and information presented in this book may not be accepted equally by all readers. The specific patterns under which bargaining occurs vary from state to state, and quality of performance in specific bargaining settings will always vary, too. Inequality is part of the scene, and contracts are built in pursuit of the remedy. After all reservations have been set forward, the rationale for increasing knowledge on the what-is-it level of active participation in public employment collective bargaining is still defensible.

Alternative ideas and arrangements are discussed. The field lacks much of the precision and certainty which we have attributed to some of the natural science areas. Some personal views may be present, but in all cases I have tried to clearly label them as such, when they occur. To keep the narrative flowing, a minimally intrusive format for references cited has been selected, but enough authoritative material has been used and identified that a curious reader may readily find sources within which to pursue ideas which have particular appeal.

The book has been developing in my mind during the past few years, reflecting some of my personal interests and special concerns in the public school work settings. A debt of gratitude is owed to the University Regents. An appointment as a Faculty Development Fellow provided the time for much of the work. The University of Nebraska at Omaha Senate Research Committee was a source of additional support. The professoriate of my department, Educational Administration and Supervision, courteously allowed their schedules to be revamped during my absence from teaching. To professors Petrie, Naylor, Kennedy, Kellams, and Burton I acknowledge that special debt. And, to Miss Inga Ronke, for typing services extraordinary, go my sincere thanks.

Robert C. O'Reilly
Professor of Educational Administration
University of Nebraska at Omaha

xii

Chapter 1

THE MEANING OF LABOR RELATIONS

The Current Situation

Collective bargaining among public employees has burgeoned since 1960. This is true for at least two reasons. First, the relative numbers of public employees is growing at a rate faster than private nonagricultural employment. From 1953 to 1970, state and local public employment rose from 8.6 per cent to 14.0 per cent of all nonagricultural employment. It is projected by the U.S. Department of Labor that by 1980, this latter figure will reach about 15.0 per cent--or nearly a doubling in about thirty years. Of that increase, educational employment rose by about 145 per cent; state and local noneducational employment increased at a nearly 80.0 per cent rate. For purposes of understanding the relative positions of the employment sectors, those figures can be compared with a 33.0 per cent gain for the nonagricultural private sector of the nation's economy.[1] To describe this in another way, there are over 37,000 counties, townships and school districts in America. All are public employers. When the host of municipalities is added, a truly impressive picture of the magnitude of public employment settings begins to emerge, and that picture does not include states in the totality of political subdivisions as employers. The picture is a conservative one, at that.

The second contributing reason can be found in the enactment, in state after state, of legislation enabling public employees to establish a union or association for bargaining purposes. Without regard to limitations on categories of eligible employees and demands--and both vary substantially from state to state--more than thirty states had passed such legislation by the mid-seventies. Some states without statutory enablement have allowed public employee collective bargaining. Illinois is the prime example, in terms of volume

1

of people and dollars involved. Illinois' position would appear to be sound, both socially and politically, in the sense that executive orders issued by different Presidents during the 1960s and aimed at federal employees have consistently supported the concept of employee organizations. There is specific case law behind this practice, too. Nevertheless, public employee groups continue to seek specific statutory endorsement of bargaining rights in every state.

With the pronouncement by the United States Supreme Court in the National League of Cities v. Usery (1976), it appears increasingly unlikely that some collective bargaining statute providing for national uniformity in the public employment sector will soon be enacted. Bills to that effect had been offered for the past several years, in both the House and the Senate. Lack of such a federal statute will not decrease the volume of activity in public sector bargaining, however. It is clear, too, that even in the wake of NLC v. Usery, some employee organizations--notably, the National Education Association--will continue to push for a federal bargaining statute. There is every indication that collective bargaining will continue to grow as more categories of public employees are brought under the jurisdiction of state laws, or with the passage, eventually, of a federal law.

Since the passage of the National Labor Relations Act (Wagner Act) in 1935, the federal government has been active in fulfilling its responsibility to insure industrial peace in the private sector by establishing laws which define employee and employer rights in the labor-management relationship. Subsequently, other legislation has been passed to meet specific needs that have arisen since the passage of the Wagner Act. The federal labor laws now in effect cover employees in private industry only, and therefore there are about 11.8 million state and local public employees not included under uniform federal legislation.

Definitions of Labor Relations

Comprehensively, labor relations has been defined as dealing with everything that affects the individual worker or groups of workers as they relate to the employer. It involves anything which may affect the employee from the time of job interview until job leaving. This definition covers all relationships, including such things as recruiting, hiring, placement, training, discipline, promotion, layoff, termination, wages, salaries, overtime, bonuses, education, health, safety, sanitation, housing, recreation, working hours, rest, vacation, unemployment, sickness, accidents, old age, and disability. This definition holds the collective bargaining process to be only a part--and a small part, at that--of the labor-management processes.[2] In this view, the contract itself is viewed as a "charter" to a comprehensive view of the employment setting.

An opposing view is that labor relations encompasses only union-management relations. In this narrower viewpoint, it is assumed that the written agreement reached between the workers and their employers is the basic labor relations code for that particular group. Some observers stipulate that because of the legal requirement that the agreement between union and management be written, and because the agreement can be enforced either by a court or through arbitration (if that method of enforcement is written into the agreement), the typical American labor agreement is a complete labor relations code, whole unto itself.[3] In this view, the contract is the end-all; the contract content is the limit of employment setting considerations.

From the private sector, an older agreement between the United Automobile Workers and General Motors contains a clause which is a good example of the concept that the labor agreement is a complete code of relations between management and union for the period of time covered. Literally, and in spirit, it has found its way into many other agreements throughout the United States.

> The parties acknowledge that during the negotiations which resulted in this agreement, each had the unlimited right and opportunity to make demands and proposals with respect to any subject or matter not removed by law from the area of collective bargaining, and that the understanding and agreements arrived at by the parties after the exercise of that right and opportunity are set forth in this agreement. Therefore, the Corporation and the Union, for the life of the Agreement, each voluntarily and unqualifiedly waives the right and agrees that the other shall not be obligated to bargain collectively with respect to any matter referred to, or covered in this Agreement, or with respect to any subject or matter not specifically referred to or covered in this Agreement, even though such

> subject or matter may not have been within the
> knowledge or contemplation of either or both of
> the parties at the time they negotiated or signed
> this Agreement. [4]

The Bible is one source to consult for an understanding of the human condition. From the well-known story of Adam and Eve we know that various kinds of relations developed between the two. Doubtless, some were delightful, some were dreadful. If not a major focus, labor relations was undoubtedly included. Who was to do exactly what, and what return that person received for the labor, must surely have been an immediate source for conflict, tension, and creative growth. Labor disputes are an inevitable part of the social and population growth process. Tensions form within the laboring force. Every element which gives some promise to settle those tensions and disputes is part of labor relations.

Recognizing that the term may be studied and utilized narrowly, there is value in a more comprehensive approach to understanding the term, labor relations. In a comprehensive understanding of labor relations, the following points in the total industrial relations system must be considered.

> 1. The politico-economic matrix which surrounds employer-employee relations; the industrial structure of the country; the characteristics of the labor force; the looseness or tightness of the labor market; management's personnel policies; and the balance of power in the political system.

> 2. The characteristics of the trade unions; whether workers are organized by plant, by craft, or by industry; whether the power resides mainly in the local or national unions; the degree of membership attachment; the strength of union finances and leadership.

> 3. Trade union tactics; whether the labor relations program concentrates mainly on controlling the employer through collective bargaining or on influencing government through political action.

> 4. The structure of collective bargaining; the size of the bargaining units; the subjects regulated by agreement, the duration of agreements; the methods

of resolving disputes over the application of the agreement; the use of strikes; and other forms of economic pressure.

5. The framework of public control, which determines what the parties may bargain, and what tactics they may use. [5]

Historical Development of Labor Relations

Clearly, labor relations has been with us, and with us. In an historical treatment, where is the starting point? In one sense, arbitration implies labor relations, even though it is antecedent to labor relations. Arbitration is the oldest known method of settlement of disputes among men. Solomon was an arbitrator, even though in that instance of child ownership, he was far afield from labor relations. The techniques and specifics of labor relations are somewhat ambiguously together and then apart, from one time to another. Without intent to demean the development of labor relations in any single country, but for better understanding of a particular readership, the focus here is upon the American scene.

The present status of the American worker--the American employee--is the envy of workers over the world; but it did not just happen without effort. It is a result of many factors, including personal sacrifices and dedication on the part of many individuals who have devoted themselves to enhancing the worker's position. Simply put, labor relations is the struggle of workers for higher wages and better working conditions. The history of labor relations has been influenced by such varied factors as employer attitudes, economic conditions, technological changes, and governmental policies which either helped or hindered in the drive to develop more sophisticated labor relations.

After the industrial revolution, workers were "herded" into factories. Viewed from today's perspective, working conditions were frequently terrible and in some situations reached a point where workers combined with others in an effort to fight exploitation. At the same time, employers found cultural and legal bases from which to counteract worker pressures--to keep workers under control in order to protect capital investment. Thus, the labor-management tensions which comprise the industrial labor relations picture began to come into sharp focus.

The first craft unions were mainly concerned with uniform wages and conditions of employment. The philosophy of the craft unions was to get for the worker the best possible wages and conditions. From those improved wages the individual worker could then provide for himself and his dependents the medical services, pensions, and similar benefits which today are considered as "standard" fringe benefits within the total compensation package, in both the private and public employment sectors.

The craft union dealt with employers singly, or in a geographical area for a specified industry. It acted as a contractor for the workers. Consequently, it had a need to monopolize the service of its members. Each craft union controlled the quantity and quality of its members' services, thereby making its bargaining more effective. Guild and union membership was limited by high fees, arbitrary rules for entering apprenticeship, or by the difficult skills needed to perform the job. [6]

In their drive to improve their own wages and working conditions, workers have vacillated in their affiliations. At times they have sought to advance their interests under the shelter of a union; on other occasions they have sought to promote their goals through joining political parties. In actual practice, these are not mutually exclusive endeavors, but historically, they are exclusive in the relative emphasis given to one or the other activity--union or political. It is only in fairly recent times that unions, themselves, have included political action as one of four or five basic missions.

In the latter 19th century, union membership seemed to go up in times of economic growth, but declined, and political parties flourished, in times of recession. [7]

As workers organized, their unions were more or less successful. From among many, three have been selected for cursory examination here, and as examples of union activity. Each became a national union; one dropped from sight, unsuccessful over the long haul; they were of unequal size and wealth.

In the 1870s there developed a need for a larger organization than had previously been developed. It was needed to cope with the competition from immigrants, the hostility of the courts, and the unsympathetic attitude of government at all levels toward labor. The Knights of Labor was formed to unite all categories of workers into "one big union." After briefly flourishing, the Knights disappeared because it appeared that the union had a greater concern for social reforms than for wages and working conditions. It finally lost worker support as a result of its inability to provide tangible results for its members.

Later in the 19th century, the craft unions were organized under the leadership of Samuel Gompers into the American Federation of Labor (AFL). This "union of unions" clearly held in the forefront its narrow concerns for promoting increased wages and improved working conditions for its members.

During the 1920s and later came the big thrusts in industrial mass production. The need arose to develop a union to meet the needs of a growing class of industrial workers, i. e. , those not affiliated with crafts. Under the leadership of such men as John L. Lewis, the Congress of Industrial Organization was formed in 1938. The CIO followed the general organizational pattern of the AFL, except that it promoted industrial unionism, and worked mainly for the interest of the unskilled and semi-skilled workers. The bitter rivalry which developed between these two unions seemed to have a stimulating effect upon their organizing efforts. [8] Now, in the latter 1970s, the American labor scene is dominated by the combined AFL-CIO with George Meany as its long-term, 80-year-old patriarch. The differentiation of guilds, crafts, and unskilled has been lost in the larger union.

Government Attitude and Labor Relations

During the 1890s, when corporations were growing rapidly, employers were able to obtain court injunctions prohibiting strikes. After all, the rights of capital were deeply ingrained in the culture. These injunctions served as a disrupting influence on unions; imminent jail sentences for union leaders were frequently the consequences for ignoring the injunctions. Federal troops and state militia were used to restore order and protect non-union workers brought in by management as strike breakers. The generally unsympathetic tone of the courts can be seen in a minority viewpoint expressed by Oliver Wendell Holmes after the Supreme Court of Massachusetts enjoined peaceful picketing in <u>Vegelahn v. Guntner</u> (1898).

> One of the eternal conflicts out of which life is
> made up is that between the effort of every man to
> get the most he can for his services, and that of
> society ... to get his services for the least possible
> return.... I can remember when many people
> thought that, apart from violence or breach of con-
> tract, strikes were wicked, as organized refusals
> to work. I suppose that intelligent economists and
> legislators have given up that notion today. I feel
> pretty confident that they equally will abandon the
> idea that an organized refusal by workmen of social
> intercourse with a man who shall enter their antago-
> nist's employ is unlawful.

This view, that strikes and associated non-violent activities should be lawful, has come to prevail with regard to
private industry. It is not as widely accepted a view, however, in the public employment sector. Many states which
allow public employees to bargain also have no-strike laws
for (some) public employees.

During the 1920s, a change in public opinion favored
labor over management, and made politically possible the enactment of the Railway Labor Act. Corporations had become
increasingly powerful. Suffrage had been extended; it became evident to the general populace that the worker needed
legislative protection. The Railway Labor Act of 1926, although limited in scope, required employers to bargain collectively, and gave railroad workers the right to form unions.[9]

During the 1930s three different labor laws were passed
which affected the scope of labor relations by establishing
guidelines from which the rights of employees could be defined. The Norris-LaGuardia Act prohibited the federal government from issuing injunctions in labor disputes. It out-
lawed "yellow dog contracts" and limited the liability of unions
for unlawful acts by their officers and members.[10]

The Wagner Act, or the National Labor Relations Act
of 1935, gave workers the right to join unions and elect
their own collective bargaining representatives--in the private
sector. The act established not only the right of employees
to self-organization, but also provided them with the machinery for holding elections to determine the union preference of
the majority of the employees, and provided exclusive bargaining rights to employees to organize without employer interference.[11]

The Wage-Hour Act, or the Fair Labor Standard Act of 1938, was established to regulate minimum wages, overtime pay, and child labor laws. The law related to interstate commerce and the production of goods marketed for interstate commerce. This statute established a minimum wage of twenty-five cents an hour during its first year, thirty cents an hour for the next six years, and forty cents an hour at the end of seven years.[12]

Union membership during this period of time expanded, partially as result of a favorable attitude toward labor by government. The greatest growth was among the unorganized, semi-skilled workers in the mass production industries. Under the protection of the government, unions grew strong and powerful. And, predictably, the insensitive exercise of that power by some unions laid the political groundwork for reactionary or compensatory legislation which came in the 1940s.

A series of amendments that were attached to the Wagner Act became known in 1947 as the Taft-Hartley Act. One major provision of that bill was to define unfair labor practices. Principally, the statute was designed to equalize the collective bargaining power between employers and unions; in effect, this was a curb on the power of unions. This act also provided that when the health and safety of the nation was endangered, the President could obtain an injunction halting a strike for 80 days.[13]

The Landrum-Griffin Act, or the Labor-Management Reporting and Disclosure Act of 1959, was designed as a labor reform act, to provide for the reporting and disclosure of certain financial transactions and administrative practices of labor organizations and employers. The act gave union members the right to participate freely in meetings, to ballot secretly, and to have access to financial and business records of their unions.[14] This act was government's notice to the unions that it was becoming increasingly involved in establishing and enforcing rules and regulations aimed at maintaining the rights and safety of the worker. Abuses of power by some large union organizations signaled the need of some workers for protection from their own large and remote organizations. The act also set forward the national policy for collective bargaining. Section 7 provides as follows:

Employees shall have the right to self-organization, to form, join, or assist labor organizations, to bargain collectively through representatives of

their own choosing and to engage in other concerted
activities for the purpose of collective bargaining
or other mutual aid or protection, and shall also
have the right to refrain from any or all such activities except to the extent that such right may be
affected by an agreement requiring membership in
a labor organization. . . .

Clearly defined limits and requirements have been developed by statutes and cases to structure the collective bargaining process. Although this and all previous labor legislation was specific to the private sector, the process itself
has been the nucleus for each of the many statutes which
have been enacted in state after state since the latter 1950s,
and which are aimed specifically at public employment.

Labor Relations in Public Employment

Labor relations for public sector employees are no
less complex than in the private sector. The scope of allowed negotiations is generally defined by statutes, but these
are specific and different, state by state. Occupational categories included in a given statute may differ from those in
any other state's statutes. So, too, may the negotiable
items vary. Generally, wages, hours, and other terms or
conditions of employment or professional service are allowed.
In a University of Hawaii study of seventy-five state statutes,
municipal ordinances, and professional regulations bearing
upon public sector labor relations, it was found that only
one-third provided for grievance procedures in the agreements written under those statutes, ordinances, or regulations. One-fifth of those laws permitted parties to proceed
with negotiations in the event of impasse; i. e. , the parties
could continue in "regular" negotiations while the routines
for resolving impasse were also in motion. Typically, these
laws authorize public employers to negotiate collectively in
the settlement of grievances arising under the terms and
conditions of employment, and to negotiate and enter into
written agreements in determining terms and conditions of
employment, including wages and hours. Legislative approval
is not necessary, but is advantageous to public sector bargaining. Agreements may be required to extend over a
period coinciding with the budgeting period of the state. [15]
The original statute which provided bargaining for teachers
in Nebraska is a good example. Passed in 1967, the
Teachers Professional Negotiations Act stated that contracts

could be written for more than two years, and at that time the legislature met every two years.

Of the statutes examined, less than one-third contain some provisions regarding union security. Most provide for employer deduction of dues upon employee authorization. 16 Nearly 90% of the seventy-five statutes, ordinances, and regulations contained some measure regarding the determination of appropriate units; i. e., how may a public board recognize the appropriate union? Most of the state statutes provided for administrative agencies which were authorized to determine criteria for the identification of bargaining units. 17

Much of the umbrella of governance under which labor relations are conducted is constructed in court cases. Two recent pronouncements from the United States Supreme Court are excellent cases in point. In the National League of Cities v. Usery (1976), it was decided that the Congress lacked the power to extend the minimum wage and overtime provisions now binding in settings of private employment to cover state and local government employees. Labor Secretary W. S. Usery, Jr. was the federal government's defendant in an unsuccessful attempt to implement this Congressional enactment.

In the Hortonville School District v. Hortonville Education Association (1976), the major finding was that in states which statutorily prohibit strikes by public employees (and that is nearly every state), and in situations where they strike nonetheless, employing boards of trustees may dismiss the striking employees without violating the individual rights assured in the Constitution. Each of these cases, and particularly the latter, has a number of qualifying circumstances attended in detail in the Court's decision; but each, obviously, bears heavily on labor relations generally. The magnitude of this last statement becomes apparent when it is recognized that, as the National School Boards Association has stated, forty-five of the fifty states have vested the power of personnel dismissal in local boards.

It is necessary to emphasize at this point that certain cultural, political, and social intangibles are woven into public employment labor relations. In speaking to the representatives at the National Education Association meeting on June 30, 1974, Association president Helen Wise said of collective bargaining:

Our comprehensive bill for all public employees,

> introduced and supported by the Coalition for American Public Employees, is making significant progress in the House and Senate. It is interesting to note that as we push the one bill, that when enacted will make situations like Timberlake and Hortonville history, the AFT consistently opposes this legislation. 18

Her statement points up the lack of unity within organized labor generally and public employment specifically. Those intangibles which sometimes become manifest in rivalries and hostilities fragment the power of any group--and labor history is full of such events.

At the same time that President Wise's (1974) advocacy seemed to portend a positive climax for a federal statute long-sought by the public employment sector, it must be candidly observed that the Court's action in Usery seems to have halted hope. Yet, the narrow margin (5-4) of the court's decision, and some other factors, indicate that pursuit of such a political goal may still be practiced.

Another NEA speaker, President John Ryor, made the following comments at the 1976 Association's Representative Assembly:

> On June 24, the Supreme Court of the United States, by the narrowest of margins, 5-4, struck down Congress' authority to extend minimum wage and overtime provisions to state and local government employees.
>
> This decision was the sixth consecutive anti-public employee ruling handed down by the current majority of the court. In the five earlier decisions, a firefighters' union was denied dues checkoff, and the court approved; a police officer with permanent status was fired without a hearing, and the court approved; a police department imposed a strict dress code including specific rules on grooming, and the court approved; a firefighter was fired for moving outside the city limits of the city for which he worked, and the court approved; teachers in Hortonville, Wisconsin, were fired for striking, and the court approved.
>
> And now the current majority on the court has

extended itself even farther, removing the right of public employees to gain protection from wage and overtime abuses by state and local government employers.

But this decision does more than that. It also strikes at the very core of the power of Congress to act on a federal collective bargaining bill for state and local government employees, including teachers and faculty. [19]

As indicated by Ryor's comments, public employment includes diversity in occupational categories. The extent of the diversity can be seen vividly in, for example, a single school district which may maintain distinct labor relations with two employee categories--those demanding certificates from the state department of education, and "others." Even though the certificated employees would typically account for 75% of the dollar costs in this labor-intensive enterprise, a brief look at the "others" should clarify this diversity factor in public employment.

Among the "others" there may be subdivisions into several groups. The district may bargain with a food service union, a custodial union, a licensed engineers union, a skilled crafts union (e.g., bricklayers, steam fitters), and so on. Most administrators agree that there are advantages in keeping to a minimum the number of unions with which bargaining occurs. They include:

1. less call upon time for bargaining;
2. less opportunity afforded each union for comparisons;
3. more stability in handling grievances and in contract administration, generally.

There is a direct relationship between the number of bargaining units and the size of the government unit; as the size of the unit grows, so also does the probability of diverse bargaining units.

For full understanding, such employment diversity within a single employing unit must be seen against the larger backdrop of the many employing government units-- a state and all of its political subdivisions. Coupled with existing national organizations of county commissioners, city council members, mayors, and school boards--each of which

Table 1. 1

Major Public Employee Unions[21]

Organization Name	Employee Type	Affiliation	Approximate Size
American Federation of State, County, and Municipal Employees (AFSCME)	all public workers	AFL-CIO	700, 000 members
American Federation of Teachers (AFT)	teachers	AFL-CIO	450, 000
Fraternal Order of Police (FOP)	police	none	over 300 locals
International Association of Fire Fighters (IAFF)	firefighters	none	160, 000
National Education Association	teachers	none	2, 000, 000
Service Employees International Union (SEIU)	building maintenance personnel	AFL-CIO	*500, 000

*Of the 500, 000, about 35% are public employees.

has certain cultural, political, and social biases of its own--
the full complexity of public employment labor relations begins
to emerge. Add to these considerations, pressure; money
pressure, and many other, more subtle, pressures. Ryor,
in his address to be teacher representatives, continued:

> Our drive for federal collective bargaining stan-
> dards, and for minimum wages, for overtime pro-
> tection, and for all of the other rights so basic to
> citizens of this country--that drive is still on track.

We are going to achieve equitable collective bargaining legislation for all teachers and for all public employees. We have already done so in thirty of the fifty states. And we are going to do so in Colorado, in Texas, in Alabama, in Virginia, and in Missouri and Ohio and Kentucky, and every single state in this union. And the results and the power of those successes are going to gain us the eventual goal of uniform minimum standards for collective bargaining for all teachers and for all public employees. [20]

Tensions will continue. Statutorily endorsed public sector labor relations seems probable of extension. To prevent or reduce acrimonious relations between the employees and those administrators who stand for the public board or council, new levels of understanding labor relations must be achieved.

Table 1. 2

*Contract Settlements in 1977[22]

Employer Category	Location	Increase	Term of Contract
general employees	Rock Island, IL	1977-78: None but COLA, quarterly	1 year
	San Diego, CA	1977-78: 5%	1 year
fire fighters	Albany, NY	1976-77: 5. 5%	1 year
	Smithfield, RI	1977-78: 7%	2 years
		1978-79: 6%	
police	Antigo, WI	1977-78: 6%	1 year
	Hull, MA	1976-77: 5%	
		1977-78: 5%	2 years
teachers	Brawley, CA	1977-78: 5. 5% plus 2. 7% special salary increment	1 year
	Boise, ID	1977-78: 12. 5%	2 years
		1978-79: 5. 5%	

*No fringe benefits are shown in Table 1. 2.

Graphically, some dimension of collectivized public employees and of public labor relations can be seen in the accompanying tables. Many smaller but viable unions are not included in Table I. Many unions which primarily service private employment are excluded; e. g., the International Brotherhood of Teamsters claimed nearly 100,000 members in public employment.

Table 1.2 is a display of recent contract settlements, by categories of public employees.

References

1. Ehrenberg, Ronald G. The Demand for State and Local Government Employees. Lexington, MA.: Lexington Books, 1972, p. 1.

2. Roberts, Harold S. Roberts' Dictionary of Industrial Relations. Washington, D. C.: Bureau of National Affairs, 1976, p. 157.

3. Seyforth and others. Labor Relations and the Law in the United Kingdom and the United States. Ann Arbor, MI.: University of Michigan, 1968, p. 99.

4. Bureau of National Affairs, Inc. Collective Bargaining, Negotiations and Contracts. Washington, D. C.: The Bureau, 1964, pp. 20:346-347.

5. Reynolds, Lloyd G. Labor Economics and Labor Relations. Englewood Cliffs, N. J.: Prentice-Hall, Inc., 1970, p. 292.

6. van de Vall, Mark. Labor Organizations. New York: Cambridge University Press, 1970, p. 1-3.

7. Industrial and Labor Relations, A Core Curriculum of Related Instructions for Apprentices. USOE, ERIC Document Ed 116 033, 1975, p. 23.

8. Ibid., p. 24.

9. Roberts, op. cit., p. 270.

10. Industrial and Labor Relations, op. cit., p. 25.

11. Roberts, op. cit., p. 274.

12. Ibid., p. 106.

13. Ibid., p. 274.

14. Industrial and Labor Relations, op. cit., p. 26.

15. Najita, Joyce M. Guide to Statutory Provisions in Public Sector Collective Bargaining: Scope of Negotiations. Honolulu: University of Hawaii, March, 1973, p. 1-2.

16. Najita, Joyce M. and Ogawa, Dennis T. Guide to Statutory Provisions in Public Sector Collective Bargaining: Union Security. Honolulu: University of Hawaii, May, 1973, p. 1.

17. Ogawa, Dennis T. and Najita, Joyce M. Guide to Statutory Provisions in Public Sector Collective Bargaining: Unit Determination. Honolulu: University of Hawaii, June, 1973, p. 1.

18. National Education Association. Proceedings of the Representative Assembly, 1974. Washington, D. C.: The Association, 1974, p. 9.

19. National Education Association. The Advocate, September, 1976, p. 7.

20. Ibid., p. 7.

21. Eaton, William J. A Look At Public Employee Unions. Washington, D. C.: Labor-Management Relations Service, 1970.

22. Labor-Management Relations Service. "LMRS Newsletter," August, 1977, p. 6.

Chapter 2

ELECTIONS, DEMANDS AND NEGOTIATIONS

Introduction

There are many similarities in the ways that collective bargaining is carried on in any of the types of political subdivisions. This is not to suggest that personnel problems in a school, for example, can be better solved when a mayor or city council decides to intervene in behalf of a local school board or district superintendent. To the contrary, experience suggests that each agency does best when limiting its efforts to its own bailiwick. But the similarities of public employment conditions indicate that a great deal can be learned from considering the larger picture.

Partially because public bargaining is a new field, local units or unions have typically sought to find bargaining representatives from within the local group. Very large locals have hired professional representation. The vast majority of such public employee locals are not large; as noted earlier, the teacher's local in the New York City Public Schools, representing nearly 70,000 employees, is unique, and within the 700,000-member American Federation of State, County, and Municipal Employees (AGSCME), most locals are small. The same is true of the National Education Association locals. Locals composed of non-professional employees have sometimes sought professional negotiators from their national group; however, local professional unions (e. g., teacher unions) typically have carried out their own bargaining endeavors, with some assistance from state and national offices.

The NEA has traditionally held a philosophical position against being called a labor union. For purposes of collective bargaining, its posture is parallel to that of the

American Federation of Teachers, or any other organized employee group. It is convenient, and functionally accurate to think of all such groups as unions.

Labor Department reports for the end of 1976 indicated that the total of all U. S. workers in unions was 22, 463, 000. Although that membership represents about ten per cent of the nation's total population, it also reveals a decreasing union membership; in 1974, the total exceeded 22, 900, 000. To some extent, the power to hold elections, present demands, and carry through negotiations is affected by the number of union members.

Differentiation among employees on the basis of identifiably differing employers has sharpened recently, as the National Labor Relations Board (NLRB) has considered and pronounced. Private schools employing teachers have been exempt from statutes under which teachers in public schools have organized. Not being public employers, such schools have been differentiated from public school districts. Now, the NLRB has ruled itself into the controversy, and has asserted that it should control the bargaining interests of teachers in parochial schools, which are, by definition, private enterprises. The assertion is based upon the argument that the dollar flow in such schools is so large that it affects private enterprise. Not really settled because of some ambiguities by the NLRB, the question of privately employed teachers organizing and bargaining in a pattern similar to that of public school teachers will doubtless be extensively litigated.

Choosing the Bargaining Unit

Deeply ingrained within the American ethic is the concept that "the majority rules." This concept has been carried into the process of choosing a bargaining unit. Where there are organizations competing for the right to represent a group of workers at the negotiating table, the organization garnering a majority of votes generally will be granted this right.

Most state statutes have already authorized 'exclusive' representation rights which give the organization with authorization to represent the majority of employees in the appropriate bargaining unit the right and the duty to represent all employees in that unit. [1]

A brief sampling of existing statutes which address the topic of choosing the organization which will represent the employees of a unit reveals both similarity and difference. From Connecticut, the 1965 Act Concerning the Right of Teachers' Representatives states:

> Any organization or organizations of certificated professional employees of a town or regional board of education may be selected in the manner provided herein for the purpose of representation in negotiations with such boards with respect to salaries and all other conditions of employment. A representative organization may be designated or elected for such purpose by a majority of all employees below the rank of superintendent in the entire group of such employees of a board of education or school district or by a majority of such employees in separate units. (Section 10-152b)

With a decade or more of experience in public sector bargaining upon which to draw, Iowa passed a more comprehensive statute in 1974. It covered all public employees in the state. Within the Iowa Public Employment Relations Act, the legislature spoke to the topic of elections, in detail.

> 1. Upon the filing of a petition for certification of an employee organization, the board shall submit two questions to the public employees at an election in an appropriate bargaining unit. The first question on the ballot shall permit the public employees to determine whether or not such public employees desire exclusive bargaining representation. The second question on the ballot shall list any employee organization which has petitioned for certification or which has presented proof satisfactory to the board of support of ten per cent or more of the public employees in the appropriate unit.

> 2. If a majority of the votes cast on the first question are in the negative, the public employees shall not be represented by an employee organization. If a majority of the votes cast on the first question is in the affirmative, then the employee organization receiving a majority of the votes cast on the second question shall represent the public employees in an appropriate bargaining unit.

> 3. If none of the choices on the ballot receive the

vote of a majority of the public employees who could be represented by an employee organization, the board shall conduct a runoff election among the two choices receiving the greatest number of votes.

These selections from Section 15 of the Iowa statute stand as good examples of the Iowa legislature's determination to leave little to chance, to be extremely mandatory.

Although this part of the Iowa statute is strongly dependent upon the rule of the majority concept, the preceding section of that Act allows an employing board to recognize, for purposes of exclusive bargaining representation, an employee organization which has as members at least thirty per cent of the employees of the unit.

Not only legislation, but also reports of research into unique organizational problems provide helpful insights into the topics of election and recognition. A case study of the impact of the movement to unionize prison personnel in Ohio is a good example. Ohio lacks a collective bargaining statute for public employees. Negotiations have led to contracts, but the case law basis for such action does not preclude multiple unions in single job settings. To help end union rivalry, the state's Department of Administrative Services developed guidelines for union recognition. The executive branch has been the active agent for public employment collective bargaining. [2] Similarly lacking legislation, in 1971 New Mexico's attorney general delivered opinions that public employees could bargain, and that state's personnel board issued the necessary regulations. Some states stipulate negotiations; some call for "meet and confer." These selected statutes and situations reveal some differences between states, some differences within a state (depending upon specific conditions) and at the same time, confirm the earlier stated truism about the need for majority support.

In its infancy, organized labor was consistently frustrated by the stand of management, the position of the courts and, generally, government hostility. From the founding of this country until the 1930s it was almost impossible for workers to choose a bargaining unit. From a legal point of view it was not allowed, as indicated in an early legal observation:

The hostility of the courts was first given vent in the criminal conspiracy doctrine. This doctrine,

> "imported" by the American courts from English common law at the turn of the 19th century, was unbelievably narrow by modern standards. The doctrine flatly concluded that combinations of workmen to raise wages were criminal conspiracies and hence illegal ... the shadow of the conspiracy doctrine hung heavily over organized labor throughout most of the 1800s.[3]

The rights of public employees have paralleled those of private labor. Regarding union membership for teachers, a Chicago court said in 1917 that "... it was inimical to proper discipline, prejudicial to the efficiency of the teaching force, and detrimental to the welfare of the public school system."[4]

Schools would not hire teachers who were union members, and teachers who were organizers were dismissed from their jobs. Inasmuch as organizing must precede election and recognition, such attitudes were effective deterrents. Now, that issue has apparently been resolved with the ruling in McLaughlin v. Tilendis (1968), a circuit court decision. That court declared that the First Amendment rights include the rights to form and join a labor union, and that the Civil Rights Act of 1964 provides remedy for employees who are dismissed because of their exercise of Constitutional rights.

There is no reason to believe that any court would now rule differently in a similar suit coming from some other category of the public employment sector; McLaughlin and Steele (his colleague) were teachers in Illinois.

The state statutes on election vary. Obviously, if elections do not conform to prevailing statutes, they may be open to question, with the possibility that they may be overturned in court. In order to assure the integrity of bargaining unit elections, an outside party might be called upon. The American Arbitration Association has suitable resources, and is especially capable of handling the plethora of details associated with a representation election. In order to be adequately prepared for an election, the following questions must be answered:

> 1. Who will be eligible to vote? It may be helpful in answering this question to list those clasifications of employees who will be ineligible to vote. Consideration must be given to long-term substitute

employees, contract employees on official leave, etc.

2. When will the vote be held? On what day and during what hours will the polls be open? What will be the date of run-off election if one becomes necessary?

3. Where will the polling places be located? Junior and senior high schools are logical locations because they are strategically located throughout the district and usually have ample parking facilities. Where there are competing unions, one of the unions may argue for polling places on the basis of the location of its membership. The expense of establishing a polling place in each school is usually prohibitive. Polling places at locations other than the schools provide a satisfactory arrangement.

4. Who will be the election clerks at the polls? How many official observers from each organization on the ballot will be allowed at the polls?

5. What procedure will be used to list eligible voters, identify voters, challenge ballots and resolve the challenges?

6. What safeguards will exist to protect the secrecy of the ballot?

7. What shall be the wording of the question to be presented to the eligible voters on the election machine or paper ballot?

8. In what order will the choices be placed on the ballot? This can be determined by the flip of a coin. The ballot should provide for a choice of "no organization" as well as for the choice of the organizations, by exact title, seeking to represent the employees.

9. What vote is necessary to win the election?

10. What notice of election and sample ballots will be given?

11. How may an absentee ballot be secured and

voted by employees on leave, absent from work
because of illness and for other reasons?

12. Where, when and by whom will the final tally
be held?

13. Who will be the final arbiter of any disputes
concerning electioneering irregularities or the tab-
ulation of votes?

14. Who will bear the expense of the election?

15. For what time period will the results of the
election cover? If no bargaining representative is
elected, when may another election be held? If a
bargaining representative is elected, when and under
what conditions may another election be held?[5]

Once a union or association has been recognized as the
bargaining agent, it must be determined for how long that
union will represent the employees. There may be a statutory date for termination or renewal. There may be a contractually agreed upon term. Clearly, both employer and
employee share in the necessity for time control over the
"life span" of a representative bargaining unit, and that must
be balanced between too short and too long. Many statutes
call for annual renewal--year-by-year-proof--of the representative status.

The election and designation of a specific bargaining
unit occasionally needs clarification in each local setting.
Two cases heard before the Nebraska Court of Industrial
Relations serve as good illustrations of both latitude and constraint. In the matter of the City of Grand Island and the
American Federation of State, County and Municipal Employees, AFL-CIO (1971), certain conclusions were pronounced. It was the city's desire to bargain with one unit.
The employees wanted occupational differentiation; i. e. ,
clerks, firefighters, electrical workers, and so on wanted
each to be in their own union. With no statutory directive
stipulating the necessity of a single union, the court found
that workers may organize according to occupational categories, and governing boards must recognize each after elections have been held according to law.

In the International Association of Firefighters, AFL-
CIO v. the City of Fremont, the Court of Industrial Relations

(CIR) was asked to determine those employees who should be excluded from representation by virtue of the fact that they represented management. That is, the fire chief was excluded by mutual agreement, but what about such job titles as fire captain, fire marshal, and fire lieutenant? A study of job descriptions led the CIR to exclude captains and marshals, but to allow the inclusion of lieutenants in the union because they were principally firefighters and assumed other duties only in the absence of a captain.

Elections, in and of themselves, may not determine the constituency of the union. Objections to inclusiveness may be voiced by rank and file; or, as in the firefighter dispute, by the governing board, which in this instance was a city council.

Proposals and Demands

After election comes recognition. After recognition comes the first step in the bargaining process, the presentation of proposals and demands to the board. The written list of proposals and demands is a formal presentation, characteristically done at the time required by the statute of each particular state.

This initial effort in the bargaining process rests upon a mutually accepted concept of good faith. This means that the parties will deal with each other openly, fairly and sincerely, from the time of initial contact until the contract is signed. It is a troublesome concept, not perfectly matched with the adversarial setting.

In the private sector, the National Labor Relations Board (NLRB) and the courts have built an extensive set of conditions for bargaining:

1. There must be a serious attempt to adjust differences and to reach an acceptable common ground.

2. Counter proposals must be offered when another party's proposal is rejected. This must involve the "give and take" or an auction system.

3. A position with regard to contract terms may not be constantly changed.

4. Evasive behavior during negotiations is not permitted.

5. There must be a willingness to incorporate oral agreements into a written contract. [6]

Failure of any of the above can become grounds for allegations of unfair labor practices because of lack of good faith.

Although good faith bargaining receives severe tests during the entirety of negotiations, it is an integral part of the proposal and demand phase, particularly. It is a term of relativeness; it abhors extravagance and exaggeration. How substantial, then, should the demands be? Should the union demand a twenty per cent pay raise? Is that extravagant? What is the scope of proposal and demand which is within both the desires of the union and the concept of good faith? In anticipation of compromise, there is a tendency for both sides to exaggerate their position. Within such a planning framework for the entire bargaining session, proposals and counterproposals come to the verge of violating the concept of good faith.

Proposals and demands generate counterproposals. Compromises may emerge. Acceptance of positions must occur between the union and the governing board as the collective bargaining process operates. Confront, revise, reject, accept--these become the reactionary postures to the proposals and demands. Proposals are not developed in anticipation of immediate and total acceptance by the other side; they are written offers of position aimed at developing discussion. It is pointless, then, to make a proposal which involves an area of interest in which a public board is proscribed from negotiating. Although these items vary from state to state, the following list includes items commonly considered non-negotiable.

1. Items not directly affecting the welfare of members of the negotiating unit.

2. Items with a primary function of determining educational policy (in schools).

3. Items which may encroach directly upon an area inherent to management, such as the hiring of personnel. [7]

The formulation and preparation of the proposals is

customarily the responsibility of the persons who have been chosen or hired as employee representatives. These proposals, however, should come from the "grass roots"--from the nurses, firefighters, laborers or teachers who comprise the local union. As a normal part of the preparation aspect, the employee representatives are expected to screen and refine the various proposals as they are gathered.

As soon as the concerns, desires, and priorities of the constituency have been identified, the written preparation of the proposals should commence. The proposals should be designed to support improved conditions for the membership.[8] Some proposals will need to be written out in full. Proposals in the form of amendments to existing contracts need only state those words which require changing or omitting. Others may simply require the rewriting or clarification of an already established policy. Under no conditions should these proposals be silly or ridiculous, flippant or insincere; all should be as sensible as they can be made by the employee representatives. Revisions and amendments must be set forward with understanding of their meaning as one goal.

The demands, or proposals, if wisely formulated by the union, will conform to one or more of some such major union functions as union security, wage and effort bargaining, individual employee security, or contract administration. Examination of numerous letters containing proposals and demands made by public employee unions to their employing boards reveals that the major interest is the wage and effort category. For example, for teachers that would mean the continuation and extension of the single salary schedule. Even though recognizing that such schedules do not create vested rights, teachers have found that they provide an excellent base from which to approach the initial wage demand. These schedules are not without advantage to the employing board, for they provide a base from which to start the budget planning process. Some data base is necessary because negotiations are conducted with relative goals in view.

Similarly, information which employees or employer groups may use in speaking to their particular case may be found in inter-occupational comparisons.

The data from Table 2.1 can be interpreted to mean several different things, depending upon the interests of a particular spokesman. For the city manager, reporting on the personnel budget to a city council, the perspective might

Table 2. 1

Inter-Occupational Salary Comparisons
Over Five Years, 1968-1972[9]

Occupational Group	Average Annual Rate of Increase
Maximum annual salary scales	
Police	8. 3
Firemen	8. 0
Teachers	5. 8
Minimum annual salary scales	
Police	7. 4
Firemen	7. 3
Teachers	5. 5
Consumer Price Index	4. 6

be that salaries indicate very strong compensation plans, by several comparisons. On the other hand, the data would very likely carry a different message to the bargaining team for the local teachers' association.

Many public employees are civil servants. Where does the civil service fit in the public employee bargaining setting? Civil service has a long history as a job protection device. It satisfies one of the concerns of organized workers, and civil servants who are organized may find conflicts in negotiations. The use of the spoils system, and the job insecurity which such partiality promoted, caused employees to search for some technique which would remove government jobs from arenas of political corruption. Providing continuity and stability in the services being performed, civil service has advantages from several viewpoints. Legislatures, from time to time, have expanded the coverage of employees in that category. With the passage of time, civil service has tended to become overburdened by its own bureaucratic attempts at impartiality; included employees may find that the bureaucracy itself has become a stumbling block to goal achievement through collective bargaining. [10]

It was the several Executive Orders which were sequentially issued by the three Presidents of the sixties which so sharply accelerated the extension of public employment bargaining. Ironically, those orders, allowing for the organization of federal employees who were civil servants, applied to employees already enjoying some of the benefits which have always been major goals of unions. It was not a perfect fit. In job settings other than the federal civil service, it has become apparent that the overlay of collective bargaining on civil service merits special study because it is really a new and different kind of worker organization.

In its brief history, public sector bargaining has taken on several of the practices of private bargaining; e. g., the negotiating teams meet, discuss, and recommend or decide, privately. The scope of that bargaining has steadily grown, for demands and proposals tend to accrue and extend. Policy determination through contract construction has become a real problem. Should open meeting laws be applied to bargaining? Should the press be invited to attend?

Negotiations

Negotiations are bargaining; bargaining is negotiations. Sides are identified and adversial roles are assumed. In order to assure that those adversial feelings do not attach to personalities and hamper job performance in the instructional setting, public school governing boards are well advised to consider third parties who are outsiders to the classroom setting. In negotiations, cool calculations must meet cool calculations.

Job performance protection must be attended; bitter feelings which may be aroused through disputes at the negotiation table must be kept separate from work settings. An organization in which, because of its smaller size, the union representative is also an employee in close work relationship with the administrator designated as the board's negotiator is bound to have trouble. The carryover from the bargaining table to the work setting, developed as a side effect in that earlier conflict, cannot be conducive to desirable job productivity. On the other hand, if there is substantial "organizational distance" between the negotiators for each side, their coming from within the same organization should not be counterproductive to the organization's work mission.

In those cases where common sense dictates that the

public board should employ an outsider, and designate that person as negotiator, to whom should a board turn? Where is such talent to be found? Many boards have turned to the ranks of attorneys, attracted by their familiarity with adversarial roles.

Some research indicates limitations upon negotiations in which boards are represented by outsiders. Over a three-year period, from a single state sample of negotiating school districts, those not reaching contract agreement ranged from 8 to 14 per cent. Among the group going to impasse, exactly half of the boards had employed attorneys as spokesmen. Among those boards reaching settlement and not going to impasse, attorneys were spokesmen for only about 15 per cent of what might be termed "successful negotiating."[11] Other boards have sought assistance from within other professional groups. For example, college professors from such fields as communications, administration, and economics have represented boards on occasion.

This situation calls for additional comment. First, it should be pointed out that although the boards may have protected the work setting from crippling hostilities by hiring outside, single-purpose representatives, those outside representatives have not been particularly outstanding in bringing the bargaining to settlement and contract short of impasse. Second, the procedure is in sharp contrast to predominant practices in the private sector because the magnitude of the employment particular to each specific public bargaining endeavor is likely to be much, much smaller than in a private sector counterpart--if indeed, it is even fair to think that there might be a counterpart. Public bargaining does not yet have that centralized characteristic in which a single union is involved with a representative of many employers, such as the United Auto Workers bargaining with the Ford Motor Company.

For all the problems, there is good reason for "third persons" to be used in public bargaining. The most knowledgeable persons are to be found among the professional mediators, arbitrators, and conciliators. When matched against the fantastically sharp rise in public employment bargaining over the past decade, the number of such available professionals is so small that they would be unobtainable to most boards, given even the most optimistic view of a public board's financial situation and professional negotiator inclination. Simply put, qualified third-person negotiators are in short supply.

Over the next few years, public boards will likely continue to use their own administrators on special short-term assignment as negotiators, or they will hire nearby and available professionals of one sort or another who appear reasonably suitable to the task. Obviously, special direction, qualifications, and limitations must be made explicit by the employing board and accepted by the negotiator. The board must assure itself that job performance conflict is not being built through the negotiations process. Either arrangement, with the "insider" or the "outsider" as negotiator, could be quite suitable and strongly supportive to the positive development of labor relations and enhancement of the organization's work mission, but whichever is chosen, its particular potential frailty must bear intense scrutiny.

These comments on one aspect of the collective bargaining setting have been focused upon the individual who works as the board's negotiator, not only because that position merits some analysis on its own, but also because there is greater flexibility in selection to that position than in the union's representation. This is so because, with but very few exceptions, the finances behind the typical public governing board substantially exceed the resources of the local union. Within the private sector there are many unions with awesome financial resources; to date, that is not true of most public employee unions. The union, then, has fewer alternatives than the board; it will have a local expert, who may sometimes also be an executive secretary of the local. More often than not, the union has no options--its representative will come from its ranks. Very likely, that representative will develop his or her bargaining skills through educational programs sponsored by state or national organizations. Proposals set forward for negotiation typically have merit of their own, but the level of success with which they are handled at the table is heavily dependent upon the performers in the negotiations setting, too.

How large should the employee group be when a board decides to hire an outside negotiator? It is quite a temptation to revert to numbers and declare that if a public board is bargaining with a unit representing 500 members, it should select from its own administrative staff a member to be designated as negotiator. Approached in a slightly different way, it is likewise tempting to declare that if its personnel budget exceeds four million dollars, the organization may use its own personnel, and feel confident that the adversary relationship of the bargaining table will have no job performance repercussions. But, really, should it be 500? How about 250? The truth is that this decision cannot be made by the numbers. Local public boards must be sensitive, assess their own situation, then use the particulars of the situation as the decision-influencing factors.

Demands and proposals are sometimes made at inflated levels in order to expand the parameters of consideration. In public employment settings where there are elected boards, this technique may have more value than is initially apparent. That is, it is such a transparent ploy that the other side will readily recognize it as such. For public boards that have an intense interest in the financial welfare and morale of their employees, there is also an electorate which must be addressed. Boards must face two ways. Strategically it may be clumsy, but politically it may be wise to propose to the outer parameter, then fall back to a compromise to which the other side may point with pride.

When it is time to go to the bargaining table, there are a number of tactics to consider. It is often wise to come to the first meeting with a great number of proposals reflecting problems of concern to the constituency. By preparing a large number of demands, many different segments of the membership can be satisfied; and, also, these demands allow room for negotiation. As necessary back-up to such tactics, substantial preparation is essential, with data supportive of each demand and some knowledge of the cost and impact of each demand. [12]

With the start of bargaining, concessions are made, positions are changed. Some modifications come through the form of the counterproposal. A counterproposal has been defined as "... a formal reaction to a proposal or counterproposal by the other party and may be made at any time during the course of negotiation."[13] It may be used merely to balance the other side's demands. For example, if a union proposed some sort of reduction in the work week, a counterproposal may be that if the union's proposal is accepted, a specified number of paid holidays would have to be eliminated. [14]

Counterproposals are as necessary as demands and proposals. They, too, are designed to allow room for bargaining. If used properly, counterproposals can supply the negotiator with a reasonable defense and at the same time contribute to the continuation of that very necessary two-way line of communication. [15] They are, in effect, a kind of proposal.

The equity of pay problem has long been a problem in private industry. There, as a result of the great power in such unions as the UAW, unskilled workers have come to receive as much or more for their labor than skilled craftsmen in many other settings. In public employment, political patronage becomes a force mitigating against differentiation of pay. It is a factor which inevitably is considered as any public board considers settlement. The political patronage factor is one consideration which results in relative underpay for top personnel and overpay to personnel who are unskilled or who have little responsibility. Public employee strikes in such cities as New York and San Francisco and publication of salary levels of unskilled employees which reveal inequities have caught the attention of observers of the public employment scene. [16] When municipal sanitation workers receive starting wages of $18,000 annually, and public school teachers in the same locale start at $9,000, the equity of pay problem stands out, and one influencing factor is political patronage.

The thread running throughout the entire process of proposal and demand negotiation must be good faith. Not particularly susceptible of precise definition, good faith can be subverted by either side--a violation of both the spirit and the letter of typical collective bargaining laws. Good faith does not necessarily mean that the parties will come to agreement. Impasse may still be a consequence of negotiations which are conducted in good faith. And, unfortunately, to confuse the situation even further, it must be admitted that on occasion settlement may be a consequence of negotiations in which one or both parties used deception, subterfuge, or some other bad faith characteristic.

Hard bargaining does not indicate lack of good faith. In fact, it has been stated that:

> If the state courts ... adjudicating public employment disputes adopt reasoning similar to that developed in the private sector with respect to good faith bargaining ... a government employer may bargain hard; and unless its offers to a union are flagrantly unreasonable or humiliating, it will not be found guilty of refusing to bargain in good faith.

Collective bargaining does not imply capitulation to all union

demands. Even in the private sector, where the employer
has no responsibility as guardian of the public welfare, there
is no implication that capitulation to union demands is the
only indicator of good faith.[17] But, for the process of collective bargaining in public employment to prevail, good
faith--genuineness and sensitivity--must be present as proposals and demands find their way to the negotiations table.

Although negotiations may appear to be a clear-cut
procedure, areas of vagueness do occasionally arise. In
the Madison School District v. Wisconsin Employment Relations Commission (1976), the Supreme Court reversed WERC
and declared that an open meeting of a school board could
not become, arbitrarily, a meeting for purposes of negotiations. At that board meeting, the Madison teachers' union
representatives had addressed the board on a contract provision calling for a fair share fee. Negotiations were deadlocked on this provision. At that meeting, a non-union
teacher gained recognition and spoke to the board for himself and others, contending that no such fee should become
a part of the contract. The teachers' union charged that,
by allowing such remarks, the board entered into negotiations with another teacher group, something it had agreed
not to do at the time of the union's recognition. The Supreme Court ruled that in open meetings any citizen may
enter into a discussion of the public business.

Taken together, the accompanying map of the United
States (Figure 2. 1) and Table 2. 2 reveal a good bit about
the dimensions of elections, demands, and negotiations. The
map is divided into four major areas, balanced by the number of states per area. With information derived from several sources, * comments about the two displays are appropriate.

---

*The materials for the figure and table came from four
sources. The map was produced by the Labor Management
Relations Service.[18] The four map areas and Column 7 of
the table came from Newby's Collective Bargaining....[19]
Column 6 of the table came from the Census Bureau's Characteristics of the Population.[20] The remainder of the table
data came from a survey conducted among the 55 city areas
having a population of at least 250, 000.[21] Of that group,
39 replies were received by the Bureau of the Census.
The combined data confirm the likelihood that in some states,
some large city areas still might have no collective bargaining agreements with any eligible employees.

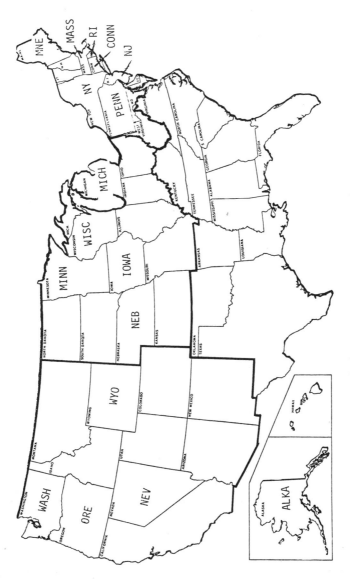

Figure 2.1--United States by Four Areas

Table 2.2

Collective Bargaining Incidence in
Large Cities, Shown by Regions

Region	Number of States	Number of States Reporting	1970 Data		Population of Reporting States (in thousands)	1977 ASBA Survey
			Number of Agreements	Number of Covered Workers		Collective Bargaining as a regionally rank-ordered management concern
1	2	3	4	5	6	7
East	13	6	114	411,850	47,564	1
Midwest	12	7	89	143,599	46,409	1
South	13	7	28	14,842	35,915	12
West	13	5	55	42,199	29,430	1

Seventeen states are identified in larger type to indicate that as of the summer of 1977, those states statutorily provided for binding arbitration for all or some of the public employee occupational categories. Those seventeen states had a population of over 77 million in July, 1976.

The map is divided into four regions--East, Midwest, South, and West--which is a kind of regional balance. Those regions are used to represent the findings from research conducted by the Bureau of Labor Statistics into some conditions of public collective bargaining as they existed in 1970; these are shown in Table 2. 2. Table 2. 2 is augmented with information from other sources, and the augmentation has implications for the larger scene of collective bargaining among public employees.

The history of public sector bargaining is very short, and the 1970 survey was conducted in its infancy, so to speak. The 1970 data showed that most of the bargaining activity occurred in the eastern U. S. , and that there was no substantial connection between gross population of a region and the number of public employees covered by contracts. The last column reveals continuation of a condition. In a 1977 survey conducted for the American School Boards Association, teacher elections, demands, and negotiations leading to contracts were still low participation activities in the South. This was in sharp deviation from every other region. The map (Figure 2. 1) provides a further demonstration of why that sharp regional difference prevails.

References

1. Nolte, M. Chester, ed. Law and the School Superintendent. Cincinnati: H. W. Anderson Co. , 1971, p. 214.

2. Standahar, Paul D. "Prison Guard Labor Relations in Ohio, " Industrial Relations, May 1976, pp. 177-190.

3. McConnell, Campbell R. Elementary Economics: Principles, Problems, and Policies. New York: McGraw-Hill, 1969, p. 627.

4. Nolte, M. Chester, and John Linn. School Law for Teachers. Danville, Il. : Interstate Printers, 1963, p. 187.

5. Nolte, loc. cit., pp. 215-217.

6. Taylor, Benjamin J., and Fred Whitney. Labor Relations Law. Prentice-Hall, 1971, p. 332.

7. Wollett, Donald, and Robert H. Chanin. The Law and the Practice of Teacher Negotiations. Washington, D. C.: The Bureau of National Affairs, 1974, pp. 1:25-32.

8. Duryea, E. D. and others. Faculty Unions and Collective Bargaining. San Francisco: Jossey-Bass, 1973, pp. 46-48.

9. "Teachers Receive Smaller Increases than Policemen, Firemen," Negotiations Research Digest, April 1974, pp. 15-16.

10. Wellington, Harvey H. and Ralph K. Winter. "Structuring Collective Bargaining in Public Employment," Yale Law Journal, 1970, p. 861.

11. O'Reilly, Robert, and Doug Nollette. "Negotiations, Impasse, and Settlement," Nebraska State School Boards Association Bulletin, April, 1976, pp. 9-10.

12. Wollett and Chanin, op. cit., p. 3:7.

13. Igoe, Joseph A., and Douglas Flynn. The School Board Negotiator. Albany, N. Y.: Thealan Associates, Inc., 1972, p. 71.

14. Nierenberg, Gerald I. Creative Business Negotiations. New York: Hawthorn Books, Inc., 1971, p. 18.

15. Koerner, Thomas F., and Clyde Parker. "How to Pick a Bargaining Team and What to Teach It," American School Board Journal, May, 1969, pp. 29-30.

16. Feurin, David. "Collective Bargaining Impacts on Personnel Administration in the American Public Sector," Labor Law Journal, July 1976, pp. 426-436.

17. Weitzman, Joan. The Scope of Bargaining in Public Employment. New York: Praeger, 1975, p. 15.

18. Labor-Management Relations Service. LMRS Newsletter. August, 1977, p. 1.

19. Newby, Kenneth A. Collective Bargaining--Practices and Attitudes of School Management. Washington, D. C.: National School Boards Association, 1977, p. 25.

20. U. S. Bureau of the Census. Characteristics of the Population. Bul 159-A. Washington, D. C.: Superintendent of Documents, 1973.

21. U. S. Bureau of Labor Statistics. Municipal Collective Bargaining Agreements in Large Cities. Bul. 1759. Washington, D. C.: Superintendent of Documents, 1972, pp. 1-2.

Chapter 3

FACT-FINDING, MEDIATION, AND ARBITRATION

Problems in the Words

All of the activities which comprise negotiations may not produce a contract; they may end in a stalemate, i. e., in impasse. If neither side is willing to accept the last offer of the other, or if only one side is unwilling, an impasse may be declared. Declaration of impasse occurs either by those who are representing the employers or by the representatives of the employees. Disputes or stalemates which arise at other points in labor-management contacts are not customarily designated as impasse.

States which have public sector collective bargaining laws provide for some next steps after bargaining impasse occurs. When that has been said, however, variety of routine in those next steps become the rule, and uniformity the exception. For example, functions which are described as fact-finding in one statute may well be called mediation in another. Even when state statutes are very similar in definitions of terms for resolution of impasse, the sequence of events may be exactly the opposite.

It is impossible to discuss impasse resolution in public employment using definitions which are specific in wording or in identification with a place and statute. The common resolution techniques are fact-finding, mediation, and arbitration. If one treats them in one way, in which their definition and sequence are harmonized with some state's statute, the terms may be slightly out of phase with their use in another state. Reconciliation to specific localities is not a large task, but the reader will need to do it if impasse is to be clearly understood.

Impasse has proven to be particularly troublesome in

certain realms of dispute, and current negotiations with some police locals provide good examples. The day-by-day activities of today's police officer may include race riots, attacks on officers, an obligation to enforce unpopular drug laws, and violence in the streets. Given a lack of new tactics to deal adequately with such events, and with many problems in the "gray area, " young police want to negotiate more than just a wage settlement. [1] Given the reluctance of most public boards to broaden the scope of negotiations voluntarily, it is easy to see a police employee/city-council employer impasse in just such a setting. Similar high stress conditions occur in other occupational settings. In such circumstances, the function of the neutral third party may be governed more by sociological-psychological factors than by the generally accepted structural bounds of such terms as fact finder, mediator, or conciliator.

Public opinion polls have consistently verified a prevailing sentiment which expects uninterrupted services to the public by public employees. Among the routines by which public employment disputes have been resolved, so that services can continue, are fact-finding, mediation, conciliation, and arbitration.

Fact-finding

Fact-finding is a procedure by which a qualified neutral person or persons make written findings of fact and recommendations for resolution of a bargaining impasse. This procedure attempts to provide an acceptable alternative to the use of economic or political force in resolving disputes between employers and employees. [2] The recommendations characteristically are not binding, but can often be used successfully to settle an impasse through persuasion and a new presentation of facts.

The process of fact-finding often becomes a means of determining certain basic parameters within which the parties may adopt a common base from which to continue bargaining. Or, the fact-finding recommendation might be written in such a way as to induce the parties to reject it and reach their own agreement. In still other situations, the process is used to do what the parties cannot do themselves. They may be in agreement, really, but they need someone else to "impose" the settlement, i. e. , to speak it. Or, they may need the fact-finder's recommendations to convince the public, the legislative body, or the union membership which might have ultimately to ratify the agreement. Yet another variation is the recommendation needed to save face with one's own team; e. g., a union that has promised its constituents too much and cannot back down without losing the faith of the membership, or a mayor who does not want to back down on a point when it will cost him supporters, even though he knows that the "price" of a settlement is small in labor relations terms.

Nearly all states that require collective bargaining in the public sector require fact-finding, either as a strike substitute or as a means short of a binding third-party solution, to avert a strike. In states where limited use of the strike by public employees has been allowed, courts generally require exhaustion of fact-finding as a condition precedent to a strike--or an injunction will be issued against the strikers upon request.

Historical Perspectives on Fact-finding

Fact-finding has a short history. As a labor dispute settlement technique, it is much more widely used in the public than in the private sector. In 1954, Michigan adopted a statute authorizing fact-finding in public employment. As late as 1965, the only states with fact-finding laws for public school teacher/board of education disputes were Michigan, Massachusetts, and Wisconsin. Since then, at least nineteen other states have provided for fact-finding for all or some groups of public employees. Where no state law applies to fact finding, local ordinances may be found which apply. In other instances, fact finding has been made available through its enumeration as one of the matters of contract, developed by way of collective bargaining between the public employee's organization and the employing board. Wisconsin is one state which provides that local governments, including school districts and municipalities, may establish their own fact-finding procedures. [3]

One reason that fact-finding is seldom used in the private sector is economic. The strike, a labor weapon for the past several decades, puts an economic bite on management, and it is very effective in influencing the resolution of an impasse. This technique is not effective in education because teacher strikes are, in the main, illegal in most states. Too, there is no really urgent economic pressure with a strike in education because the only losses are days of instruction. In most cases when teacher strikes, legal or illegal, have occurred, the days lost have been made up later. Therefore, "nothing" is lost during a teacher strike. To some extent, and because public employees are typically involved in extending a service rather than developing a product, this lack of economic pressure from striking employees prevails throughout all of public employment. However, for those occupations in which the timely delivery of the public service is important--as with nurses, police, and garbage-sanitation workers--the strike has impact, even if it is not economic.

Fact-finding and Public Bargaining

Given that even the accepted spelling varies from "fact finding" to "fact-finding" to "factfinding," it obviously follows that experts in the labor field cannot readily agree what it is. The Public Employee Relations Act (Senate File 531) of the State of Iowa defines fact-finding as "... the procedure by which a qualified person shall make written findings of fact and recommendations for resolution of an impasse." The Illinois Education Association defines fact-finding as

> ... the investigation of a dispute or impasse existing between an employee organization and an employer by an individual, panel, or board which issues a report of the facts and issues involved, and makes recommendations for settlement. 4

Some of the fundamental disagreement is over the question of whether fact-finding is essentially mediatory or judicial in nature. The process has not suffered in spite of these disagreements, which is testimony to its desirability on the labor scene. It is probably most accurate not to attempt to characterize fact-finding as either judicial or mediatory, but to recognize that the role of the fact-finder varies depending on many circumstances, including those which follow:

1. the statute under which the fact-finder operates,

2. the agency which is responsible for the administration of that statute,

3. the fact-finder's own abilities, inclinations, and values,

4. the nature of the issues in dispute,

5. the desires and bargaining skills of the parties at impasse,

6. the sequence of fact-finding, as related to other impasse resolution techniques,

7. whether the fact-finder is an individual or one of several operating as a panel,

8. the timing of the fact-finder's intervention. [5]

It is generally accepted that fact-finding is one of the steps used in impasse resolution procedures. The steps in impasse procedures, though varying from state to state, typically include some form of mediation, fact-finding, and arbitration, but not necessarily in that order.

It would be unfortunate if the parties at impasse relied upon the fact-finder to determine how much a governing board could afford to pay or how it must reallocate its resources gathered out of public taxation. Such decisions must be made by the parties in negotiation, and under the statutory restrictions of the state where the action is occurring. Yet, it is clear from the study of cases that negotiating parties have occasionally expected too much of fact-finding, and fact-finders have inappropriately usurped functional roles better left to governing boards, or boards have foresaken their roles in anticipation that fact-finding may "do their job" for them.

Considered as a technique, fact-finding has frequently assisted in the development of alternative solutions which can be offered as reasonable and attractive choices to bargaining parties. It is a technique through which solutions to problems can be discovered which will help the parties save face and survive institutionally. The parties can be forced to treat the bargaining process seriously if the fact-finder makes it clear that he or she is willing to identify publicly either of the parties as obstructionist to legitimate problem-solving.

In some situations which arise in the public sector with undue frequency, fact-finding can be very helpful. For example, in the teacher-board setting, some of the more common obstacles might include:

1. militant teachers insisting on unrealistic demands,

2. school boards refusing to make realistic offers,

3. teacher leadership needing help in convincing union membership that a fair agreement has been reached,

4. school administrators needing help in convincing the board that they have a fair agreement,

5. citizens who are unconvinced that a board needs additional funds to pay competitive teacher salaries. [6]

When too many items arrive at the fact-finding stage, it is a strong indication that one or the other of the parties has not really bargained in good faith. The study of a little comparative history reveals that in disputes which have gone to fact-finding, employee groups usually receive greater benefits in both wages and fringe benefits than do those groups which settled earlier and without using the entirety of impasse procedures. Indirectly, this is an evaluative observation upon the level of effectiveness with which the parties at dispute present their side of the case to the fact-finders; or, the values--or their absence--in the case, itself. Another problem is the too frequent failure by one or another of the parties to present relevant facts. Too often the parties present emotional arguments unsupported by facts, leaving the fact-finder with a paucity of facts from which to make a finding.

Analyzing fact-finding as a procedure or technique for settling disputes in public sector bargaining leads to such conclusions as the following:

1. A procedural method for defining the issues is necessary.

2. The public is entitled to be made aware of the issues between its representatives in government and the public employees involved at impasse.

3. The inappropriateness of economic weapons in the public sector requires a procedure for dispute settlement which involves third parties, but does not give the third party absolute authority to impose a settlement. [7]

It may be that, lacking authority, the fact-finding technique cannot bring sufficient pressure upon an obstinate city council, or a stubborn union. Continuation of impasse is a signal that alternative resolution techniques are needed.

Mediation

When an impasse occurs in collective bargaining, outsiders identified as neutral third parties may be called in to help settle the dispute. One resolution technique is mediation. In mediation, the neutral third party may encourage settlement through suggestion, advice, or other stimulation; this is a voluntary process and the decisions of the mediator are not binding on either party to the dispute. [8] Many states have, as part of the mediation process, some such agency as their state labor relations board, providing lists of professional personnel and serving as an appeals board.

In considering a possible sequence of activities following impasse, those activities might include conciliation, mediation, fact-finding without recommendations, fact-finding with recommendations, voluntary or advisory arbitration, and compulsory arbitration. Nowhere does the entire progression of activities exist in statute, nor is it likely to occur in totality. Comparatively, conciliation is the least affirmative and the least potent action in this gradated sequence, while compulsory arbitration is the strongest. Mediation is slightly more affirmative than conciliation. The mediator may make suggestions and procedural, or even, on rare occasions, substantive recommendations; however, because he has no power or authority, these more aggressive tactics should still be considered as minimally potent.

Some writers in labor relations feel that definitional hair splitting is not very helpful, declaring that there is only a technical difference between mediation and conciliation in that the third party has no power to make a recommendation. In practice, the terms are used interchangeably, and in practice, mediation is synonymous with conciliation. [9]

Mediation, then, is "the intervention of a third party

who lends assistance in settling a threatened or ongoing labor dispute ... or in arranging a conference between the parties where he attempts to bring about agreement. " This is all without power to make any binding decisions. In contrast, in arbitration, the parties, either by legislation or agreement, may be bound to accept the decision of the arbitrator. The essential job of the mediator is persuasion. Essentially, this service is made available to the parties in order to help them come to a voluntary agreement among themselves. The third-person mediator remains attached to a case upon the sufferance of the disputing parties. Throughout, it is understood that the parties will reserve judgment until a time of their own choosing, and at that time will determine whether to accept or disregard the mediator's advice. 10

The director of the Federal Mediation and Conciliation Service predicted in 1971 that the 1970s would be a very active period for FMCS. With over 155, 000 collective bargaining contracts at the beginning of the decade, and more to be added with extended eligibility for public employees, his predictions seemed reasonable. Further, he noted, then, that his office was receiving over 8, 000 notices of representation elections per year. 11

Mediation is not repressive; it does not dictate. It is informal, and different mediators get equally good results from different methods. There is, then, absence of a common understanding or formula by which the process of mediation brings about resolution. It is an intensely personal process, in which the mediator keys his work to looking outward and looking inward; i. e. , facing both directions while still maintaining trust.

Historical Perspectives on Mediation

In the United States, the principal mediation agency is the Federal Mediation and Conciliation Service. It dates from 1913, at which time the United States Department of Labor was created. The same legislation authorized the Secretary of Labor to mediate labor disputes and to appoint commissioners of conciliation for that purpose. That phase of the department's work expanded quickly and a division, the United States Conciliation Service, was established. Headquartered in Washington, the Service established regional offices in the principal industrial centers across the

nation. In 1947, as a result of the passage of the Labor
Management Relations Act (the Taft-Hartley Act), the Service
was abolished and an independent agency, the Federal Mediation and Conciliation Service, was established. It was largely
a concession to employer groups, observers having noted that
a pro-labor bias had developed while the conciliators were
part of the Department of Labor. In part, the new agency
was an effort to introduce impartiality.

The FMCS is an intervenor. The goal of intervention
is to break deadlocks which might lead to a strike. The
FMCS does not have to wait for an invitation to intervene;
however, it cannot force itself upon an unwilling employer or
union. As a neutral third party, the agency emphasizes the
need to assist both labor and management in arriving at a
mutually acceptable settlement.

Mediation and Public Bargaining

In recent years concern has been expressed from
many sources about the competition among mediators to obtain recognition in settling disputes. It is by no means uncommon to find both federal and state mediators, and occasionally municipal mediators as well, competing for the job
of settling a particular dispute. In private sector labor relations, such dual mediation is permitted. The mediator's
ethical code requires cooperation, at least on a pro forma
basis, but the naturally competitive drive leading toward
recognition for having produced a settlement is strong. In
some states, and with overlapping jurisdictions as a possibility, both labor and management may "shop" for that mediator who is seen as most sympathetic to some partisan
viewpoint which may be blocking settlement. In assessing
mediators as a group, it must be said that even as assistance may be sought from that group for dispute settlement,
the group itself, like many other groups, has some problems which have occasionally hampered the work of individuals
from within its ranks.

Very soon after appointment, a mediator will normally contact the disputing parties, seeking information about
the current status of the dispute. If, within a few days of
appointment, no progress toward settlement is apparent, all
parties should convene, at which time an offering of mediation services should be plainly made. Lacking legal powers
of coercion, the mediator must be persuasive--an impartial

leader and proposal analyst, bent upon settlement. Talking freely and privately with both negotiating parties, the mediator determines positions and seeks common grounds of accommodation. In joint sessions, the parties are encouraged to present their positions, and all issues may come to the table. In such sessions, passion and hostility may surface; the mediator must keep tempers down and prevent closure against new considerations. Mediation demands compromise. "There are no hard and fast rules. The role of the mediator is a rather vague and mysterious one."[12]

Mediation can be represented schematically. Figure 3.1 reveals mediation as a simplified, four-stage sequence. At Stage A, the disputants are "having at it," with both rage and rhetoric at high levels. At Stage B, the mediator has entered, diverting some attention. Requests for clear-cut statements about the dispute forces some reconsideration by

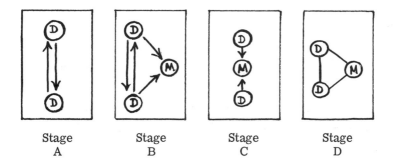

Stage	Stage	Stage	Stage
A	B	C	D

Figure 3.1--Mediation

the disputants. At Stage C, the mediator has assumed a more "in between" position. Talking to the neutral outsider has forced a more rational and more understanding stance by each disputant. Distances are being reduced. As understanding builds, Stage D arrives. Limitations resulting from the mutual impingement of demands and reality are acknowledged. The mediator can encourage discussion. The problem has become more visible, personal hostilities have been reduced, and solutions are pursued.

The concept of mediation and a general definition of it may be readily transferred from the private to the public bargaining sector. Several years ago, the National Education Association stated:

> Mediation and appeals procedures should involve the profession and boards of education in the precedents which will affect the future of public education, and assure the public, along with the profession and the school boards, that the procedures and precedents affecting the schools will be oriented to education and not to labor. [13]

Although the NEA qualified the position in additional comments, and although the position has been altering over the years, the alteration has been in the circumstance that labor and education are no longer seen as so separate, after all. With alteration over the years, the essence of the NEA's stance has found its way into many statutes bearing upon public bargaining. The NEA, representative of a large segment of the public employee group, has carried its concepts into specific procedural recommendations, stating that:

> If an impasse is reached during professional negotiation, the matter will be submitted to an Advisory Board within thirty days after the request of either party to the other. The Board will name one adviser, and another will be named by the association. A third member, who shall be the chairman, shall be named by the first two named members.
> The Advisory Board will be expected to report recommendations for settlements within fifteen days. The recommendations will be submitted to both parties and shall be made public.
> If the Advisory Board fails to make a recommendation satisfactory to all parties within the specified time, either the Board or the Association may request the State Commissioner of Education to appoint a competent individual or committee to seek to bring about a mutually acceptable settlement. The person or committee will have the authority to confer separately or jointly with the superintendent, representatives of the Board or

Association, and to utilize any other source of information. Data or recommendations may be made public. 14

In considering the specifically delineated procedures for dispute resolution, a reader who has some familiarity with state statutes on public employee collective bargaining will see that in concept and in detail, the early NEA statements have frequently become the pattern for many states and many occupational settings.

If the representatives to the negotiating table are inexperienced--and in many instances that is the case--they may know too little of the mediation process. They may not know how to work with a mediator who otherwise could assist in the last stages of negotiations and perhaps avert continuation of impasse. They may be suspicious and unable to deal with the mediator in that paradoxically open but confidential manner which is necessary. The mediator must be in the know. His purpose is to produce an agreement satisfactory to both parties without particular attention to how the settlement is reached. He does not care which party gives, or takes, as long as there is an agreement.

Arbitration

Arbitration is the settlement of a dispute by some third party, a disinterested, neutral person who hears the positions of the disputants and then reaches a decision. Usually, the arbitrator is selected with the mutual consent of the parties to the dispute. Arbitration calls for imagination and invention. Such high quality characteristics must be especially apparent in the decision, for it may be final, compulsory and binding. Any circumstance with such a dimension must be perceived as somewhat frightening by the disputants. Arbitration is the submission for determination of some disputed matter to private unofficial persons selected in a manner provided by law or by the agreement.

Historical Perspectives on Arbitration

Initial use of the term arbitration in the United States appeared in a contract involving the Journeymen Cabinet Makers of Philadelphia in 1829. (In England, arbitration was the term used to describe settlement efforts in a particular case which came from the lace trade; occurring about 1860, the technique was really more negotiation than arbitration.) In the U.S., just after the Civil War, the first labor relations umpire was employed in the settlement of a dispute between anthracite coal miners, who were members of an early union, and their employer. Occurring in Pennsylvania, the dispute arose over the affiliation itself. The United States followed England with legislation allowing for arbitrated decision-making in 1888. [15] A few years later, disputes from those same anthracite fields led President Theodore Roosevelt to apply arbitration as a settlement device. In 1922 the Arbitration Society of America was founded, and the American Arbitration Association (AAA) followed in 1926.

Many labor disputes occurred during the Great Depression of the 1930s. The AAA rejected the idea that arbitration could or should be combined with conciliation; rather, the Association saw arbitration as a strictly adjudicatory process. A factor limiting the development of arbitration during this period was the relatively small labor force; many were unemployed.

With entry into World War II in 1941 a new era in arbitration began. President Franklin Roosevelt, recognizing the need for uninterrupted manufacturing during this period, issued Executive Order 9017, establishing a tripartite War Labor Board. The functions of the Board included obligations to hear disputes that could halt work, to determine the reason for dissension, and then mediate, arbitrate, or take any other steps to settle the dispute and keep production up. The Stabilization Act of 1942 limited the Board as to what it could recommend when the disputes were wage-related. Retrospectively, the Board stated in 1945 that

> This widespread adoption, before the war, of arbitration clauses in grievance procedures demonstrates the felt need for an industrial jurisprudence adapted to the needs of modern industrial organization and practice, and proves that important segments of American industry and labor have tested and found practicable this method of making collective bargaining agreements work. The onset of war and the establishment of a no-strike, no-lockout agreement increased the urgency of the need for these procedures. [16]

Admittedly, the war provided a central focus upon which all

segments of the economy could agree. Perhaps it was even a distorting factor, but it is true that during that period of time, it became clear that a modern industrial society could maintain itself on a production-centered path, and settle labor disputes with minimum loss of man-days.

With the coming of the Taft-Hartley Act in 1947, and the Lincoln-Mills case about a decade later, the courts had pronounced the legality of binding arbitration. During that period the settling of disputes in the steel industry enhanced arbitration even further. Following litigation from the steel industry, Justice Douglas praised arbitration, saying:

> The labor arbitrator is usually chosen because of the parties' confidence in his knowledge of the common law of the shop and their trust in his personal judgment.... The ablest judge cannot be expected to bring the same experience and competence to bear upon the determination of a grievance, because he cannot be similarly informed. [17]

While arbitration is not a new concept in society, its history as a tool, refined and specific to the settlement of labor disputes, is not a long one.

Arbitration and Public Bargaining

Discussions of arbitration related to public sector collective bargaining reveal that the process is a step--the final step--in grievance procedures for the settlement of a dispute. The same can be said for impasse in negotiations; i. e., arbitration, in those states where it is a tool of resolution, is the final step which can be taken to resolve that impasse. The versatility of the tool can be seen in Table 3. 1, which is an analysis of 339 arbitration decisions occurring after contract. The research was carried out to discover the manner in which arbitration was used, as well as to determine the problems to which it was applied. Mostly used as an authoritarian or corrective tool, it was applied to such problems as insubordination or disagreements with supervisors. This analyst concluded that there is an almost complete lack of humaneness in the application of arbitration techniques in those cases where discharge or some slightly less severe discipline is the matter under grievance. The Table also shows, however, and very clearly, the versatility of the technique.

Table 3.1

Analysis of Arbitration Decisions Relating to Discharge and Discipline
Reported in Labor Arbitration Reports, May 1970 Through March 1974
by Theory of Discipline and Type of Offense[18]

	Humanitarian	Corrective	Authoritarian	Total
Absenteeism, tardiness, leaving early	2	20	8	30
Dishonesty, theft, falsification of records	2	13	28	43
Incompetence, negligence, poor workmanship, violation of safety rules	1	27	9	37
Illegal strikes, strike violence, deliberate restriction of production	0	12	19	31
Intoxication, bringing intoxicants in plant	1	10	7	18
Fighting, assault, horseplay, troublemaking	3	16	15	34
Insubordination, refusal of job assignment, refusal to work overtime, also fight or altercation with supervisor	2	42	54	98
Miscellaneous rule violations	2	20	26	48
Totals	13	160	166	339
Percent	4%	47%	49%	

As the administrator for a public governing board becomes involved in the implementation of a contract, arbitration is an obviously viable tool which can be applied to problems as they arise. The great variety of occupational categories among public employees is, itself, the indicator that the circumstances revealed in Table 3.1 are much more likely to occur among some types of employees than among others. For example, it seems unlikely that among teachers or nurses there would be a high incidence of insubordination or fighting. Yet a public hospital administrator or school superintendent might easily have just such problems arising among other employee groups in the organization.

In the public sector, arbitration may be final and binding, or it may be advisory. When final and binding, arbitration provides immediate guidance to the parties and may also point the way to future clarifications. After all, these decisions are enforceable through court order, if judicially acceptable procedure has been followed in the considerations leading to the decision. The circumstance applies to arguments which arise during bargaining, or during contract administration, or in some other phase of the labor relationship. Advisory arbitration is an intermediary step carried out with settlement as the goal; unfortunately at times, and because it is advisory, it may itself become a part of the problem which may have to be resolved by binding arbitration later. Decisions which are subject to acceptance or rejection may only extend the problem. [19]

When any argument escalates to the point that arbitration may reasonably be called for, both parties to the argument should know what arbitration will mean for their particular situation. Compulsory or binding arbitration of bargaining impasse may

1. chill negotiations,
2. separate authority from responsibility, creating a situation neither side can tolerate,
3. eliminate employer-employee decisions,
4. not guarantee "no strike. "

Final offer arbitration, a technique of forced choice, may cause

1. the elimination of unreasonable positions,
2. problem avoidance, rather than solution. [20]

Both sides should be aware that some costs are involved. Based upon daily fees as suggested by the American Arbitration Association, costs can generally be calculated. It is quite likely that the direct arbitration costs of a board-teacher dispute, for example, will be less than one thousand dollars in total. On the other hand, reluctance to settle, or dispute complexity, may extend the impasse and raise the arbitration service fees by as much as two or three thousand dollars. Few public sector disputes exceed that cost range, and the total cost generally is split, the employing board paying half and the union paying half.

Arbitration is not faultless. Some governing boards join unions in complaining that it involves too much legalism. The opinions, and even the decisions, of some arbitrators have not always been clear. Experienced arbitrators are not always available; obviously, arbitrators who lack experience are sometimes forced into service. The governing board may be surrendering some authority when entering arbitration, especially at the stage of contract negotiations. If, as in Iowa, the public employee bargaining law stipulates that as the last step in impasse resolution, arbitration shall be binding and compulsory, some authority has been surrendered, but only by state statute.

It is a fact of bargaining that impasse does sometimes occur. Disputes may also occur in contract administration. Impasse is a manifestation of controversy and conflict; it is not a sign of bad faith bargaining, nor, necessarily, of ineptness on the part of either labor or management spokesmen. Each state which has addressed public employee bargaining through statute has given some attention to resolving impasse. Definitions of resolution techniques vary by states, but after all particulars are accounted, fact-finding, mediation, or arbitration may be just the technique needed to move the adversarial agreement. The activity of a disinterested neutral is one more avenue through which the needed idea, the new expression, the unarticulated compromise which will lead to settlement, may be delivered.

References

1. Solomon, Stephen W. "California Experience: Collective Bargaining for Peace Officers," in The Role of the Neutral in Public Employee Disputes, ed. by Howard J. Anderson. Washington, D. C.: The Bureau of National Affairs, 1972, p. 9.

2. Standohar, Paul D. "Fact Finding for Settlement of Teacher Labor Disputes," Phi Delta Kappan, April, 1970, p. 422.

3. Ibid., pp. 422-423.

4. "Professional Negotiations Guidelines." Springfield, Illinois: Illinois State Education Association, 1968, p. 33.

5. Yoffe, Byron. "Fact Finding in Public Education Disputes ...," Journal of Law and Education, April, 1974, p. 268.

6. Rowmell, George T. "Fact Finding Can Unblock Bargaining Impasse," Nation's Schools, March, 1970, p. 78.

7. Hinman, S. B. "Fact Finding in Public Education ...," Journal of Law and Education, April, 1974, p. 278.

8. Gilroy, Thomas P. and others. Educator's Guide to Collective Negotiations. Columbus, Ohio: Charles E. Merrill Co., 1969, pp. 76-77.

9. Miller, William C. and David N. Newbury. Teacher Negotiations: A Guide for Bargaining Teams. West Nyack, N. Y.: Parker Publishing Co., 1970, p. 235.

10. Baerwald, Freidrich. Economic Progress and Problems of Labor. Scranton, Pa.: International Textbook Company, 1967, p. 242.

11. Indik, Bernard P. and others. The Mediator: Background, Self-Images, and Attitudes. New Brunswick, N. J.: Rutgers, the State University, 1966, p. 6.

12. Baer, Walter E. Strikes. New York, N. Y.: American Management Association, 1975, pp. 46-48.

13. National Education Association. Guidelines for Professional Negotiation. Washington, D. C.: The Association, 1963, p. 39.

14. Ibid., p. 36.

15. Pattison, George. An Outline of Trade Union History. London: Barrie and Rockliff, 1962, pp. 9-14.

16. Fleming, R. W. The Labor Arbitration Process. Urbana, Ill.: University of Illinois Press, 1965, p. 15.

17. Ibid., p. 24.

18. Wheeler, Hoyt. "The Punishment Theory and Industrial Discipline, " Industrial Relations, May 1976, p. 239.

19. Wollett, Donald and Robert Chanin. The Law and Practice of Teacher Negotiations. Washington, D. C.: The Bureau of National Affairs, 1974, p. 3:34.

20. Ibid., p. 6:85.

Chapter 4

CONTRACT AGREEMENT AND ADMINISTRATION

Completing the Agreement

As negotiations proceed and proposals, one after the other, are mutually accepted--and, perhaps, initialled by each party to indicate that acceptance--bargaining moves toward its end. Ending bargaining is the goal of the parties; i. e., to end with a set of proposals agreed by the bargaining teams, and which each team can present to its larger group, its constituency, for acceptance. For educators, agreement upon a contract comes with ratification by the board of education and acceptance by the teachers' local. Ratification and acceptance should occur at very nearly the same point in time, so that neither group can be embarrassed by untimely news releases. On occasion, such unilateral action by one group has caused embarrassment for the other, and reconsideration as a reaction to new, outside pressures.

An early--perhaps the first--negotiated agreement for teachers was in Norwalk, Connecticut. It came at the conclusion of a bitter strike in 1946, preceding laws allowing bargaining. Typically, today's agreements come more easily, but both parties need to guard against actions which may produce needless hostility.

The final negotiated agreement should be written and signed by the appropriate member of each bargaining team. It is a bilaterally established agreement. There cannot be any hidden or unwritten portion to the agreement. The agreement can be for no longer a period of time than is statutorily permissable in that particular state. It may incorporate anything to which the parties have mutually agreed, and which are not, by statute, proscribed from the bargaining table. Although some states suggest a contract format, for most

59

states the style or order of the agreement itself is whatever is locally desired. The contract may be as lean and clean or as complex and compendious as the parties mutually desire.

After the agreement has been written and signed, it should be distributed. Within its terms, it is the document which will govern labor-management relationships in that locale. If well written and sound, it should be a substantial support for the implementation of personnel policies.

A few rules apply to the construction of the draft of the agreement, and are appropriate for a board-teacher setting.

1. The school district's chief negotiator should write the final draft, and not foist that responsibility upon the teacher team; or,

2. The writing of the final draft should be turned to a small, joint sub-committee of the bargaining teams.

3. Final word entries should be available for criticism from both teams.

4. The contract form should clearly provide a space for sign-off from both teams.

5. After endorsement by the teams, outsiders should not be allowed to change the agreement.

6. Language should be examined for vague, ambiguous, or obscure words, and the agreement presented to constituencies for adoption. [1]

The Contract

A contract is an agreement to which the parties mutually subscribe. For public employees, it means that services of some sort will be provided for some specified level of compensation. It is something for something, whether it be considered in its collective form or as it applies to an individual. The form of the contract must be clear, must be legal, but the substance is what is paramount.

Some perspective on the education enterprise is

important. Education accounts for thirty-two per cent of all public employment, and more than half of all state and local government employment. Over ninety per cent of the 16,000 local school districts are independent of any other governmental unit. Local school boards exercise both legislative and executive authority--and, occasionally, judicial authority as well. Like municipalities, counties, and other units of local government, schools derive most of their income from taxes on real property, from state subvention, and from categorical grants from the federal government.[2] These political subdivisions of the state are the units with which most public sector contracts are made between employee unions or associations and employing boards or councils.

The variety of public employees makes for variety in negotiated contracts. Table 4.1 illustrates the contractual variety, as revealed by an analysis of teacher contracts. Even in a single employee category, variety surfaces, and it is also demonstrated in the extensiveness of the contracts.

Table 4.2 is devoted to another public employee group. Using a sample from an alphabetically arranged array of cities in the 250,000-500,000 population range, the first occuring six cities show the variety of contracts for police, a variety visible in both salary and working conditions. With varied employer types, varied employee categories, and a geographical spread, uniformity is clearly not to be expected in either compensation or working conditions among public employees. Contractual variety is the rule, and that realization gives rise to the need to keep local considerations alive during bargaining.

After observing the extent of contract variety which occurs in substantive items, it is necessary to emphasize that contracts, as they are to be implemented, must be stable. One way to enhance stability is through the use of a zipper clause. Over a decade ago, when public employment negotiation was still in its infancy, some writers were stressing that "... something called a zipper clause should be included in every contract. This is a guarantee that should be written into the overall package that teachers and boards agree upon."[5] A contract clause which will provide that stability and adequately close the agreement need not be long, as indicated by the following example:

The City and the Union, for the life of this agreement, each voluntarily and unqualifiedly waives

Table 4.1

(A) Teacher Contract Analysis in Six
Selected Schools in the Midwest[3]

(Current Contracts)

Schools I.D.	Size by Student Registration	State in Which Located	Contract Clauses				Salary Schedule		
			No. of General(B) Working Conditions		Preamble	Statement of Recognition	Steps	Columns	Top Teachers Salary
			Articles	Sections					
A	50,000	Kansas	19	72	Yes	Yes	14	11	16,450
B	10-50,000	Iowa	13	69	Yes	Yes	16	6	18,270
C	5-10,000	Illinois	21	96	Yes	Yes	16	5	19,278 (FY1976)
D	2,500-5,000	Nebraska	1(C)	0	No	Yes	20	9	20,832
E	500-2,500	Kansas	13	32	Yes	Yes	17	5	13,968
F	fewer than 500	Iowa	17	66	Yes	Yes	13	4	12,230

(A) Collective bargaining law enacted in Kansas - 1970; Iowa - 1974; Illinois - no law; Nebraska - 1967.

(B) Every article or section was tabulated; paragraphs were not individually counted; no article or section devoted to salary, wages, or fringe benefits is accounted in these numbers.

(C) Many or most of the working conditions are stated in the board policy book of this district, rather than in the negotiated contract.

Table 4. 2

Some Conditions of Employment for
Police in Selected Cities[4]

| Cities | Salaries | | | | Three Conditions | | |
| | Chief | | Patrolmen | | Paid | Longevity | Residency |
	Minimum	Maximum	Minimum	Maximum	Hospitalization	Pay	Reqs.
Akron	26, 270	29, 265	11, 939	13, 956	100%	Y	Y
Albuquerque	20, 115	30, 228	9, 443	13, 291	50%	N	N
Austin	- - -	27, 589	10, 212	13, 320	100%	Y	N
Birmingham	25, 688	31, 242	10, 471	12, 355	100%	Y	Y
Buffalo	- - -	29, 500	9, 980	12, 700	100%	Y	N
Charlotte	24, 300	31, 015	9, 616	12, 273	100%	Y	Y

the right, and each agrees that the other shall not
be obligated, to bargain collectively with respect
to any subject or matter referred to or covered in
this Agreement, or with respect to any subject or
matter not specifically referred to or covered in
this Agreement, even though such subjects or matters may not have been within the knowledge or
contemplation of either or both of the parties at
the time that they negotiated or signed this Agreement. [6]

An examination of similar zipper clauses leads to the
identification of some common elements which should be included in each zipper clause. They are:

1. identification of each party
2. length of the waiver
3. voluntary agreement to waive right to bargain
4. release from obligation to bargain on:
   a. any subject covered or referred to in the
   contract
   b. any subject not covered or referred to in
   the contract
5. subjects included in the waiver
6. subjects excluded from the waiver
7. statement of ample time to bargain
8. statement of good faith bargaining
9. amendment clause and time limitations
10. dates of the term for the contract.

Originally seen as a management device, the zipper
clause provides contractual stability and can be a good test
for labor, as well.

Conditions Influencing the Contract

Cost as an aspect of contract and employment deserves
more than a passing glance. Economic models and theories
have proved to be helpful tools in establishing equitable compensation in the private sector. It is economically stimulated
with a profit motive. In public employment settings, labor
costs are a substantially greater outlay than in private employment. For comparison purposes, the typical U.S. corporations spend about four times as much for employee compensation as they do for new plant and equipment. [7] Schools
are labor-intensive organizations, and typically, about seventy-

five per cent of the operational budget goes for instruction, i. e., teacher salaries.

Because public employment is in the realm of politics, it lacks the steadiness which a rational analysis of costs might provide for the private sector. Upon mandates for new educational services from the legislative or judicial branches, local educational agencies must respond, frequently in action lines which have overtones of cost. For example, consider the educational employment implications of one recent federal law.

Public Law 94-142 was enacted in 1976 as a new and comprehensive piece of legislation for the education of handicapped persons. The regulations for administration of the law were signed by the Secretary for Health, Education and Welfare in April, 1977. Section 504 of the regulations is a key portion, stipulating what services must be provided.

Besides requiring schools to evaluate handicapped children and provide them with an appropriate public education, alongside of non-handicapped children if possible, by September 1978, Section 504 states that districts must establish due process procedures for parents and handicapped children, including a notice of changes in educational programs, an opportunity to examine records, and an impartial hearing. Schools must also make extracurricular activities equally available to the handicapped and non-handicapped, pay for room, board and non-medical expenses if the district places a handicapped child in a residential school, and make "reasonable accommodation" to employ handicapped teachers.

Early litigation is beginning to provide an indication of some of the financial effects of this legislation on local school district budgets. A South Carolina school was ordered to re-admit an emotionally disturbed adolescent boy who was expelled after he attempted to engage another boy in a fight on school grounds. In Donnie E. v. Herbert A. Wood (1977) it was charged that the school district violated Section 504, which forbids discrimination on the basis of handicap, when it excluded him from school, and failed to provide for him an education tailored specifically to his needs. The district was ordered to evaluate Donnie immediately and develop an individualized plan of special education services for him for the 1977-78 school year.

Technically, those 504 requirements to test handi-

capped youngsters and give them an appropriate education
appeared to be designed to go into effect in September 1978,
with school districts simply required to make education programs accessible to handicapped children in 1977-78. However, in Mattie T. v. Holladay (1977), two Mississippi school
districts were ordered immediately to test and evaluate handicapped children individually and provide educational services appropriate to the needs of each.

The point is that legislatures mandating and courts
ordering higher levels of operational costs for programs with
very low pupil-teacher ratios will clearly affect local school
budgets. Similar extension of services is common to every
political subdivision, and bargaining parties must give cog-
nizance to budgetary implications which come with the mandated programs.

Another influencing condition is sheer numbers. Although the total population of the U.S. is increasing, and
soon will pass 220 million, the distribution of citizens by
age ranges is changing. Government agencies, as providers
of services, carry different aggregate loads as a consequence.
The total headcount loss to schools may mean a total headcount gain to welfare agencies, considering their responsibility for older citizens. In fact, there are fewer young and
more old persons in the total citizenry than there were just
a few years ago. Education, if considered as a commodity
which has been delivered without variation by public schools,
is faced with a very different problem now than it was in the
1950s and 1960s when growth was a principal argument for
negotiating instructional salary increases. The creation of
low-load, high-cost programs, as in the education of the
handicapped, may indicate the unsuitability--the untruth,
even--of the continued consideration of education as a commodity without variation. For political purposes--and others,
too--different kinds of programs may eventually call for budgetary differentiation. Some aspects of this population shift
as it affects schools are shown in Table 4.3.

Teachers who once bargained for salary increases on
the basis of increased load should be aware that that condition has disappeared and cannot now influence the contract
in their favor. It is beginning to appear that the pupil-
teacher ratio, as the indicator of load, is a fiction anyway,
given the great program differentiation which now character-
izes the educational services of schools.

The bargainers cannot possess all facts which might

Table 4. 3--School Enrollment, Staffing, and Average Salaries
for Selected Years (Public Schools)[8]

Enrollment Staffing Salaries				Data for Selected Years					
	1955	1960	1965	1970	1971	1972	1973	1974	1975
Pupils enrolled	30,680	36,281	42,174	45,909	46,081	45,744	45,430	45,056	44,700
Elementary	22,159	24,350	26,670	27,501	27,688	27,323	26,435	26,386	25,800
Secondary 1	8,521	11,931	15,504	18,408	18,393	18,421	18,995	18,670	18,900
Classroom teachers	1,286	1,600	1,933	2,288	2,291	2,332	2,369	2,387	2,394
Elementary	827	991	1,112	1,281	1,261	1,291	1,304	1,311	1,303
Secondary	459	609	822	1,007	1,030	1,041	1,065	1,076	1,091

	1960	1965	1970	1971	1972	1973	1974	1975	1976
Average salary, all teachers $1,000	5.0	6.2	8.6	9.3	9.7	10.2	10.8	11.7	12.5
Elementary $1,000	4.8	6.0	8.4	9.0	9.4	9.9	10.5	11.3	12.1
Index (1957=100)	72.7	90.4	127.0	132.2	142.3	149.1	158.7	170.6	183.2
Secondary $1,000	5.3	6.5	8.9	9.6	10.0	10.5	11.1	12.0	12.8
Index (1967=100)	74.2	90.7	125.1	134.6	141.1	147.7	155.8	168.2	180.7
Percent of teachers under $7,500	88.1	81.8	36.6	24.7	20.3	14.9	8.9	(NA)	(NA)
$7,500-$8,499	11.9	10.1	19.7	18.8	17.5	16.8	14.6	(NA)	(NA)
$8,500-$9,499		5.5	14.4	15.6	16.5	16.0	15.6	(NA)	(NA)
$9,500-$11,499		2.6	19.1	21.9	22.6	24.7	28.1	(NA)	(NA)
$11,500 and over			10.3	19.0	23.1	27.7	32.7	(NA)	(NA)

be pertinent to the agreement. But that cannot be the basis, either, for anything less than a rigorous, thoughtful, searching preparation for the frank discussions which should be the hallmark of the bargaining table.

Table 4.3 is a good illustration of one kind of information which should be at hand, available to both management and labor. It is not included here to indicate the necessity of a databank approach to the examination of alternatives, but to create alertness to the usefulness of information-- data--in defending or attacking positions taken during bargaining. Everything which is available may not be used, but it would be difficult to argue that high quality contracts are likely to emerge when the bargaining parties are ignorant, unobservant, and unprepared.

Bargainers should be aware of a wide variety of conditions which might influence the contract, as suggested in the following questions:

1. What does a trendline show about the number of persons below the poverty income level?
2. What is known about the level of unemployment?
3. How do income levels compare to previous years?
4. What is the large economic picture; i.e., what is indicated by the gross national product and the balance of payments record?

All of these questions have both national and local implications. Their effect can be refined to specific localities. They bear strongly upon a single element of the agreement-- compensation--and should give some idea of the magnitude of preparation which seems desirable, given the large number of elements in typical contracts. They reflect considerations of how the labor market works and incorporate some sense of economic equity.

Finally, it is necessary to recognize explicitly two limitations which come from the revenue-salary relationship. The development of educational programs takes money. The only budgets over which citizens still have much control are those of local political subdivisions. In many states, operational budget increases which rest upon tax levy increases must be submitted to a referendum. The 1970s have witnessed an increasing rejection rate for such referenda. If no additional revenues are available, from where will budget--

salary--increases come? The question, when it has been raised for arbitration, has been answered in different ways. In some settings, salary increases have been awarded; in others, the employees have been told to work for the same dollar rate. Local circumstances have affected final decisions. This question of support recently drew the attention of John Ryor. Speaking at Burlington, Vermont, in May, 1977, the NEA president declared that schools, finding themselves short of funds, should close rather than try to run less than a full academic program. For hard-pressed bargainers on the local scene, such a comment can not be terribly helpful. With such heavily negative tones, the statement will doubtless be viewed as a threat by many school patrons.

Acting from the same general set of premises, another union, the Assembly of Governmental Employees (AGE), has recently come forward with a paper which examines public employee productivity. The AGE pointed out to its 700,000 members that there is a money crunch. Faced with the probable continuation of lean budgets, the AGE asserted that increased productivity seemed the "least painful approach to bring revenues and costs into a better alignment." To preclude the imposition by management of unsuitable work standards, the AGE suggested an active employee role in upgrading production. Employees should assume a more creative and aggressive role with, not against, management, and move toward a common objective of doing the job better and cheaper, but without bargaining away worker gains. Sharing and cooperation are key words in the proposal. [9]

The second problem which is related to revenue has to do with the falling value of the dollar during inflation. The Bureau of Labor Statistics' Consumer Price Index has revealed an annual rise in the cost of living of from five to twelve per cent during the 1970-1977 period. Compensation at the same dollar rate, then, over successive years, really means a reduction in purchasing power in each of those succeeding years. Technically, it is important to note that the CPI is not a true cost of living index because it excludes too many costs from consideration. It is, nevertheless, a helpful reference point from which to understand cost escalation.

Administering the Contract

When ratified by the employer and accepted by the union, the contract is final and has become the official statement under which work obligations must be understood. A contract is a balance of competing interests; it is an effort to introduce stability into a situation which is inherently fraught with tension. Although most contracts are voluntarily entered by the parties to the agreements, that is not the case in collective bargaining. Justice William Douglas, writing for the Supreme Court, commented on this aspect of the labor contract in United Steelworkers v. Warrior and Gulf Navigation Company (1960):

> When most parties enter into contractual relationships, they do so voluntarily, in the sense that there is no real compulsion to deal with one another, as opposed to dealing with other parties. This is not true of labor agreements. The choice is generally not between entering or refusing to enter into a relationship, for that in all probability pre-exists the negotiation. Rather, it is between having that relationship governed by an agreed-upon rule of law or leaving each and every matter subject to a temporary resolution dependent solely upon the relative strength, at any given moment of the contending forces.

In its form, the contract is an acknowledgment of competing interests, and it is the instrument through which the difficult task of balancing and harnessing those competing interests is attempted. Experience, particularly in the recent years of public sector bargaining, has shown that management will not readily bargain all the items which might be desired by the union. This tendency to resist expanding the scope of bargainable items is management's attempt to reserve authority unto itself.

Unlike private labor relations, in public employment a public service must be performed. That is, a private corporation is not operating under some kind of legal order to deliver a service. Public employers are generally ordered to deliver their services; they are ordered by statutes, ordinances, or regulations. In public schools, the education service is stipulated by each state's legislature, in accord with the state constitution. The school board must provide the service. Especially for schools, then, contracts are not voluntarily entered. Yet, for a specified term, they are binding agreement under which the service is provided.

One way for a board to stabilize its negotiated contracts is by developing structured goals. Such goals can become criteria against which tentative agreements can be measured and evaluated. The after-the-contract goals should be specific to localities, and should include these three, broadly stated goals.

1. Awareness and acceptance of each and every article in the contract by the administrative staff.

2. Unified implementation of the items of the contract in every school in the district.

3. Individual administrators working toward operational goals of no grievances and no litigation.

This means that all administrators who have personnel management responsibilities must be close to the entire contract development procedure, advise about it, and then implement it. Teacher unions might adapt a comparable stance as a philosophical position for bargaining. [10]

Although it is desirable to approach contract administration with the goal of "no grievances," realistically it must be recognized that contracts cannot cover all contingencies, that administrators may falter, and that honest disagreements over interpretation of contract language may produce disputes. The American Arbitration Association has reported that in the administration of contracts, some disputes between teachers and boards have occurred repeatedly. Some of those repetitive disputes arise over the following questions:

1. Are substitute teachers entitled to be paid during periods of illness, on the same basis as are regular, full-time teachers?

2. Is it discriminatory to give a teacher an "unsatisfactory" evaluation rating, then transfer that teacher to another location?

3. Is it a contractual violation to assign a teacher to non-teaching tasks, not specifically set forward in the contract?

4. When teachers receive assignments during regularly scheduled preparation periods, is extra pay for lost preparation time necessary?

5. May a principal transfer an assignment as athletic coach from one teacher to another?

There are no pat answers. Each answer must be individualized within boundaries indicated by the contract, local custom, common practice, statutes, finances, and so on. Resolution techniques may include mediation, fact-finding, conciliation, and arbitration.

The services of all public employees are not needed with equal urgency. At a given instant, the need for a teacher and a firefighter is uniquely different. Settlement of disputes may be by arbitration. Or disputes may escalate to the point of work disruption, i.e., strikes, or some kind of work stoppage. To avoid strikes by such critical public service employees as firefighters and police, many states have enacted laws calling for compulsory arbitration. The senior person in American labor, George Meany, has recommended final and binding arbitration in some circumstances in public sector employment. Education is not a vital service, it is not a critical incident service in parallel to the firefighter's service. Nonetheless, arguments about the long-term effects of the instructional endeavor, the disruption of societal lifestyles, and other items have been raised in support of binding arbitration, no-strike legislation for teachers. Many states have just such laws.

Public employment contract complexity is building with the passage of time, as new contracts succeed old ones and as the accrual factor sets in. Incidences of grievance are likely to increase, too, despite increasingly sophisticated contract management. This seems likely because, from the private sector, the contractual grievance procedure has emerged as a suitable device for the settlement of disputes. Boards for the nearly 16,000 school districts can expect more, not fewer, grievances. So, too, can other public boards. But that is not the goal. Contracts should evidence such forethought, such preparation, such harmony with reality that they become a positive force in the delivery of the service for which the public agency is charged. The contracts coming from collective bargaining cannot be thought of as superseding personnel management but practically, those contracts should contribute to good labor relations.

Policy and Contracts

The logical support for the creation of policy is the same as that for any system of formal justice. Fairness demands clear statements, so that performance may be matched against mutually understood expectations of employee and employer. Policy protects both, up to a point. In the historical development of labor and management roles, the establishment and implementation of policy has been in the hands of management. In the past, boards have made the rules for teachers in the work setting.

This reservation of authority to management has been expressed in several ways. A legislature may direct a school board, as its local agent, to bargain some items and not to bargain others. Court interpretations will then further clarify and stabilize what is bargainable. Such restrictions find expression in contract management rights clauses. Typically, such clauses state that "any agreement reached must be subject to present and future laws and must also be subject to present and future policies and regulations of the board [of education]."[11] Cases of disputes have arisen out of unilateral action by which boards have made policy under such a clause and those new policies have been viewed as adverse or punitive by teachers. Boards may reasonably use bargaining as an avenue to achieve their own ends, for bargaining is a two-way street, and a contract is something for something. However, for a board to use reserved authority to make unilateral changes in work obligations, when these may be viewed as punitive by the affected employees, cannot be called wise contract administration. Some might even view such action as unethical.

In the creation of new policy by any governing board, consultation should be broad. Inquiries into affected employee groups are appropriate. Policy changes should not be retroactive. It is just such action which needlessly agitates and inflames employees. It violates the rational support for the concept of policy. It places adjudication of questions into the realm of whimsy. Strictly, adjudication must be within the bounds of fairness.

The formulation of policy should not be delegated. Statutorily, it may not be possible; historically, the policy function has rested with administration. That power, and obligation, rests specifically with governing boards, Wise use of that power can expedite the board's charge for service,

and can complement work contracts. Wise use calls for so-
licitation of advice when policy change is considered, and for
insistence upon procedural due process as a necessary protection of the standards of natural justice. Wise use, also,
insists that employees be made aware of existing policy, and
that it be applied uniformly by the administration.

The eras of arbitrary action accepted without question
by public employees have passed. New levels of self-deter-
mination have developed within the ranks of public employees,
creating constraints upon a management style which prevailed
for decades. It is merely one manifestation of the certainty
of change in any dynamic society, but it does call for reconsideration of policy, of how it is created, and why. It calls
for joint consideration of the contract and policy, as governing boards view personnel administration through contract.

References

1. "Government Employee Relations Reports." Washington,
   D. C.: Bureau of National Affairs, 1970, pp. 61:
   1006.

2. Rehmus, Charles M., ed. Public Employment Labor
   Relations. Ann Arbor, Mich.: The University of
   Michigan/Wayne State University, 1975, p. 2.

3. O'Reilly, Robert C. "Living With the Negotiated Contract." Paper delivered at Houston, Texas: National
   School Boards Association Convention, March, 1977,
   p. 5.

4. "Government Employee Relations Reports." Washington,
   D. C.: Bureau of National Affairs, February, 1977,
   pp. 71:2152-53.

5. Rhodes, A. Eric. "How to Negotiate with Your Teachers--
   Without Surrendering," School Management, September, 1966, 142.

6. Werne, Benjamin. The Law and Practice of Public Employment Labor Relations. Charlottesville, Virginia:
   The Michie Company, 1974, p. 584.

7. Granof, Michal W. How to Cost Your Labor Contract.
   Washington, D. C.: Bureau of National Affairs, 1973,
   pp. 1-2.

8. Bureau of the Census. Statistical Abstract of the United States, 1976. 97th ed. Washington, D. C.: Superintendent of Documents, 1976, p. 134.

9. "Government Employee Relations Reports." Washington, D. C.: Bureau of National Affairs, June, 1977, pp. 712:10-12.

10. O'Reilly, op. cit., p. 3.

11. Cassell, Frank H. and Jean J. Baron. Collective Bargaining in the Public Sector.... Columbus, Ohio: ERID, Inc., 1975, p. 183.

Chapter 5

INTEREST ARBITRATION

Introduction

Those philosophical and operational lines of difference which separate the bargain-dispute-settle aspects of private from public employment become glaring when the scholarly writing on the topic of ad hoc arbitration, done prior to the 1960s, is studied. In private employment, the general unacceptability of arbitrator-set salary and wage levels became apparent about the end of World War II. (It was during World War II that arbitration rose to prominence as a dispute settlement technique in labor relations.) That is, arbitrators, having once settled a general wage dispute, were seldom chosen a second time because of dissatisfaction with the settlement by either labor or management. That record was an unacceptable expenditure rate for arbitrators. Those rejection experiences led to the conclusion that arbitration of contract bargaining impasse, i. e., interest arbitration for the settlement of wage and salary disputes, should be avoided, and that binding interest arbitration should not, really, occur. Voluntary, advisory arbitration was reluctantly conceded to be a reasonable tool, but also one of last resort. This was the private sector labor relations experience.

Even with the organization of public employees during the 1960s, that same viewpoint continued to prevail among labor relations experts. Strikes by organized public employees during the 1960s indicated the error of applying the viewpoint to the public sector. As is not true in the private sector, all public services are vital, and many are time-crucial. State legislatures recognized the desirability of service continuity; they observed the history of the private sector, and they rejected that mode of contract development in which interest arbitration was relegated to the last and

/

least desirable position. For example, acting at different times, the adjacent states of Iowa and Nebraska mandated final and binding arbitration for the resolution of all bargaining impasses in the public sector. The structural forms in the two states differed but an identical goal prevailed in statute. That goal was continuity of service by public employees. By functional definition, interest arbitration was a last-occurring event in the contract settlement activities, but it was no less desirable an event than any other which the legislatures mandated upon the bargaining parties.

Iowa's legislature, coincidentally, acted at just about the right time to fit very well into earlier predictions of growth in arbitration services. One survey of arbitrators, done in 1972-73, revealed a clear expectation among the most active members of the National Academy of Arbitrators that a shortage of acceptable arbitrators would become evident within the next five years.[1] Iowa's first mandated contracts for public employees were for the school year 1976-77, and one result was a sudden burst in the use of arbitration. (Some Iowa agencies bargained before 1976, but did so voluntarily.) Arbitration came hand-in-glove with bargaining; i. e., mandatory bargaining opportunities for public employees did not occur in Iowa until final, best offer, binding arbitration was also available for the settlement of interest disputes.

An earlier chapter was devoted to a discussion of techniques for resolving disputes. Arbitration, one of those techniques, has a dual nature in that it can be used either before or after a contract. Versatility has contributed to its popularity. In 1970, public sector arbitration represented about five per cent of the total effort of the American Arbitration Association; in 1977, it was about fifty per cent.[2] Because of its growth and because of its dual nature, the topic of arbitration has been given extended coverage in this text. In this chapter coverage has been restricted to interest, or contract, arbitration; a chapter devoted to rights, or grievance, arbitration will follow.

Equity and Comparability

How much money should be paid to an employee for performing his or her service? Should it be variable from year to year, based upon an evaluation of performance? Should it be an amount which is stable in its purchasing value, linked to the Consumer Price Index? Should there be annual salary increments, keeping pace with accumulated job experience? Should pay be directly related to manpower available; i. e. , in times of personnel shortage, pay would be high, and vice versa? Should compensation be delivered in some pattern advocated by the employee group, or by the group using the service?

These few questions are presented explicitly here to emphasize the difficulties which surround any notion that a pay package will be equitable. Tensions, strains, and some inequities are inevitable, given the various viewpoints which will be brought to any collective bargaining setting. The questions also surely point to the likelihood that bargaining is the best and most viable technique yet developed through which employees and employers in a democracy can address questions of equity. It is a problem approach, and aims at resolution short of violence.

Equitable treatment consists of more than recognition that some kind of fairness, some kind of generally understood concepts, must prevail in the distribution of money paid for services. It is the question of money, however, which is the central focus of interest arbitration. What is the level of employee interest which should become a part of the contract?

Now, the general understanding, the general expectation which each citizen has upon entering the nation's work force presupposes some modest level of intelligence, including an awareness of the social and economic scene. Nurses, teachers, firefighters, or policemen can have no realistic expectation of becoming millionaires through their work. Persons in these occupational groups, when employed in public agencies, have some expectations of the money level at which their services will be compensated. Each such employee can see what standard of living can be supported through a particular occupation, and a level of expectation is built. Yet, money from any employer, public or private, is seldom given over to employees without their tugging and hauling to get it. So ... enter bargaining, dispute, and interest arbitration.

One part of the expectation among public employees has traditionally been job security. In terms of equity a trade-off occurred: higher job security for comparatively lower salaries. Financial security is one goal in the drive for equity, and for public employees, economic equity has been enhanced through uninterrupted job performance and uninterrupted compensation. But traditions change, and this concept that public employees should work for less money but have job security is obviously on the wane.

Considered as a joint procedure, collective bargaining moves toward an agreement. The agreement is produced, accepted, and ratified. Acceptance is an indicator that in the viewpoint of the majority of employees, some notion of equity must have been satisfied in that agreement. The same is true of an employing board or council. The agreement must have been seen as within the bounds of reasonableness. Those bounds were established, implicitly or explicitly, on the basis of comparability.

There are not so many factors which provide a basis for comparability as a technique, a tool used in collective bargaining generally and in impasse particularly. They are:

1. occupational parallelism
2. organizational size
3. geographical proximity
4. community of interest
5. ability to pay.

Comparability is the heart of interest arbitration. Each of the above five factors may have sub-sets developed as appropriate to particular disputes. Each factor can be developed in a display with clear reference points from which an arbitrator could develop a rationale leading to a decision and award.

Occupational parallelism means that inter-occupational comparisons are not paramount. It is doubtless helpful to know of some such comparisons, but those should not be major reference points from which bargaining impasse could be decided. For example, firefighters and teachers are both public employees, and both have work years consisting of a specific number of days. Teachers and engineers share a similar academic preparation base, and for certain tasks each may have to be licensed or certificated. Occupational similarities do not make occupational parallelism, however. In some settings, the parties at impasse may have made inter-occupational comparisons, but the rationale for such may be strained, and arbiters thus must look for something better. Teachers should be compared with teachers, police with police, nurses with nurses, and so on.

Organizational size bears upon what is comparable. Teachers, many thousands of them, are employed by the New York City Public Schools. Some school districts in sparsely populated areas have teacher organizations, and have gone to impasse from disputes at bargaining. Is a teacher organization which has enrolled twenty teachers comparable to a 70,000-member union? Is a school district with 150 pupils comparable to one with a million students? How can size differential be addressed? A brief might be presented to an arbiter in which none of the organizations used for comparison would be less than twenty per cent smaller, nor more than twenty per cent larger than the organization in which the impasse had occurred. It is extremely unlikely that a group of organizations of exactly the same size could be found and used for comparisons. Many factors enter into the determination of size. Tolerance must be allowed, and common sense applied; reasonableness must prevail. As one comprehensive factor in the comparison, including organizations sized on a plus or minus twenty per cent basis would appear to answer the test of reasonableness.

A good example of an arbitrator's problem in using comparability by organizational size arose in the matter of impasse between the City of Buffalo and Local #2651, AFS-CME. The occupational category at controversy was building inspector. The city provided a display of salaries for building inspectors in thirty-three cities. One of those cities had one building inspector; another had 211 such positions. That display showed a favorable comparison for the salaries in the home city; however, the display violated reasonableness of comparability of organizational size because of the extreme range which was included. (It also had defects on grounds of geographical proximity.) The display was rejected as the arbiter built another, and found that his comparison by organizational size presented an unfavorable salary picture for the home city. [3]

Geographical proximity is especially important as arbitrators address money disputes. Living costs which are applicable in Minnesota may be irrelevant in Florida. Proximity must be tightly held, but not so tightly that other comparison factors are lost. Some public agencies of unique size are located at great distances from similar agencies. It might be the desire of an arbitrator to limit proximity to fifty miles, or even less, but if that limitation includes no other organizations of comparable size, the proximity concept must be enlarged. This problem frequently arises in midwestern states, many of which have only two or three major cities within their boundaries. In such instances, geographical proximity has been defined regionally, reaching beyond the boundaries of the state in which the dispute occurred.

The community-of-interest factor has been used to identify subgroups of employees, and has been useful primarily in the determination of membership of a bargaining unit. Employees of a single public agency may have been separated by geography, by occupational titles, by job descriptions, organizational affiliations, and so on. Subsequently, it may be their wish to join together into a single unit for bargaining purposes. If the employing board rejects that proposal and refuses recognition of the extended membership of the organization, an interest dispute results. In a particular locale, then, the arbiter would address the questions of membership inclusion and exclusion. For example, he or she might ask, should all certificated employees be members of a single union? Or, should teachers and academic department heads be in the same union? That is, is their commonality of interest, their community of interest, so pervasive and persuasive that the inclination of the governing board should be set aside with an award in favor of the extended group? From evidence, exhibits, and discussion the arbitor would rule on questions of exclusion and inclusion of membership, defining the employee's community of interest.

There are substantial and sometimes discouragingly real differences which exist between one public agency and another with regard to their ability to pay. Differences in tax bases create differences in the revenue that can be generated. To take a common measurement unit as an example, one school district may have an assessed valuation per pupil of $50,000; another of comparable size and in geographical proximity may have but $10,000 per pupil. (In only a few states would such a difference be made up by financial assistance from the state.)

Many public agencies have tax levy ceilings which cannot be exceeded. Many are not independent taxing units. For those with tax levy ceilings, that ceiling effectively establishes a maximum gross revenue from which salaries will be paid. Of course, most public employers are not so rigidly restricted in revenue potential. Where there is budgetary flexibility which allows for the development of more revenues,

or where operational funds may be moved from one budget
category to another, or where there is not an utterly rigid
budget situation, ability to pay is likely to be a factor considered by the arbitor. Such comparisons may be historical; i.e., financial conditions may be compared over some
span of years. Or, the comparison might be a match against
similar public agencies. Ability to pay is a factor which has
been used by both employers and employees, but experience
indicates that its most frequent use is by employers, to indicate inability or limited ability to pay salary increases.

Some Newer Concepts

The history of arbitration, as previously indicated,
has been pervaded by a strong sentiment to avoid the arbitration of interests. This occurred not only because it was
chancy, professionally. Disputes which come before the contract lack the contract as a base from which to settle disputes. To avoid attempts at dispute settlement because a
conventional reference point is lacking is merely to avoid
the issue. Complex current social problems for which there
may be no traditional reference points are being tackled by
a willing and active judiciary branch; the courts see themselves as the last word on nearly every kind of arguable
point. There is no lack of precedent within the general social milieu for interest arbitration, in the sense that it calls
for the recognition of new and flexible reference points in
dispute resolution. Public utilities boards have been in the
interest arena for years, setting both wage and rate levels
with uninterrupted service to the public as a major reference
point. The organization of the public employment sector,
particularly, points up the necessity of arbitration, for all
public employees and employers share that unique obligation
of uninterrupted service. The new position from which arbiters should view interest arbitration was well summarized
in the following statement:

> Collective bargaining today is not the same pro-
> cess we knew in the post-World War II days.
> Neither is the social or economic climate in which
> it exists.... It is time to revisit the precincts
> of interest arbitration. Some new neighbors have
> moved into the area, and we [arbitrators] should
> get acquainted with them. [4]

The doctrine of comparability of working conditions

had its origin in 1862, when the Secretary of the Navy received directions from Congress to set wages of blue collar workers at a level to conform with the prevailing wages of non-government workers doing similar work in the immediate vicinity. Data from the 1960s and 1970s indicate that among employees, federal workers are paid more than their private sector counterparts. [5] The compare-and-then-"catch-up" notion apparently no longer holds for federal employees, as it did a century ago; however, the design in which the earnings of employees in comparable settings are analyzed is still valid and viable as a basis for wage settlements.

There are many problems in comparability, not the least of which is that the disputants may disagree, vehemently, on what factors should be compared, and what agencies should be in the comparison group. Admittedly, there are uncertainties, perhaps even weaknesses, but comparability has strengths, too. Workers who keep even with other workers have reason for satisfaction in their level of compensation; i. e. , they are not behind. Employers can note their position in the area's pay scale, and determine if it is adequate to support their recruitment needs. There are actually several primary referents bearing upon economic settlements which can be set forward as support for a position, and which an arbiter, serving in such an impasse, can reasonably consider as he works his way through evidence and discussion toward decision and award. [6]

Typical Interest Issues

Collective bargaining is an orderly sequence of events, each of which has to be accomplished in its own time and place. Between recognition and contract ratification several discrete events must be accomplished. One such event is the presentation by the union of a list of demands for bargaining. That list of demands may be very short or very long, but bargaining sessions proceed the list is likely to be diminished. When the parties find themselves deadlocked, and impasse is declared, the remaining items are those which must be resolved through interest arbitration. In most cases, that number will be small, but it is not unknown for it to remain a long list, too. With the advent of interest arbitration, costs begin to accrue to both parties (for it is a shared cost endeavor), and that brings increased motivation to settle each demand and decrease the number of items.

An excellent example of the extensiveness of unsettled

items can be seen in a Denver firefighters' bargaining impasse which occurred in 1972. There were twenty-three unresolved items:

1.	Pay for the union bargaining committee	10.	Hospitalization
		11.	Life insurance
2.	Call-back pay (from off duty)	12.	Minimum manning
		13.	Physical examination costs
3.	Internal salary study	14.	Line of duty injuries
4.	Job classification for drivers	15.	Salary
		16.	Pay for holidays
5.	Policy on safety equipment	17.	Vacations and vacation pay
		18.	Grievance procedure
6.	Temporary rank advancement	19.	Hours of duty and shifts
		20.	Sick leave
7.	Moonlighting time	21.	Mileage allowance
8.	Clothing allowance	22.	Sub-division supervisors
9.	Union security	23.	On duty work garments

Acting aggressively, the three-man panel, headed by an impartial arbitrator, secured settlement and withdrawal of fourteen items. With nine items remaining, the panel's job was more manageable. After hearings and examination of evidence the panel made awards, some of which were affirmations. The salient points of this case were two: 1) the unusually large size of disputed items; 2) the panel's aggressive moves toward reduction as a first step toward resolution.[7]

Arbitration and Tax Levies

Questions and uncertainties over fiscal matters have always been a factor in the philosophical reluctance of boards and councils to enter into collective bargaining. Certainly, bargaining has not been advocated from the management side in the public employment. As taxing units responsible for the gathering of revenues, local governing boards also have been traditionally responsible--exclusively--for the plans for disbursement. Should boards and councils fear a loss of control over money? How much control is lost? Does arbitration of impasse represent another or further loss of power?

Figure 5. 1 portrays a hypothetical situation in which a teachers' union and a local school board came to impasse. For purposes of historical reference, the salary agreement levels for 1976 and 1977 are shown. The dispute has been portrayed as the gap between the board's salary base offer for 1978 ($9,950), and the teachers' demand ($10,400), a gap of $450 on the base salary.

Figure 5.1

Interest Arbitration at Impasse

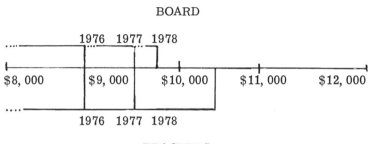

The figure is based upon the presumption that impasse occurred at the point of the $450 disagreement. A final, arbitrated settlement would not be less than $9,950 (the board's last offer), nor more than $10,400 (the teachers' last demand).

If an outside neutral party were to resolve the dispute at $10,400, the board would have "lost" control over 4.3 per cent of the proposed salary. That is, the board offered to increase the base salary from $9,500 to $9,950, a $450 increase--almost 5 percent. The teachers' demand was for a $900 increase--just a little over 9 per cent.

If, however, an arbiter were to resolve the dispute by adding $100 to the board's offer, the award would direct a base salary of $10,050, an increase of $550, or about 5 per cent. In such a case, the board would have "lost" control over about .9 per cent of the instructional salaries money.

Schools are labor intensive organizations, with about 75 per cent of the operational budget committed to instructional salaries. Most annual budgets are composed of both operational and capitalization costs. What would the $100 award mean, then, in terms of the arbitrator's influence upon the total budget of the local school? This would certainly vary from one school district to another, but the award would probably mean a financial influence exerted by an outside neutral in the range of about .1 to .4 per cent of the budget.

In a single instance, the effect is minuscule; and if a board considers that as a loss of control, the level of magnitude in the loss should be recognized. Carried on in successive years, an accrual effect would occur, and the budgetary influence of the outside neutral would increase. Typically, the services of a neutral party to arbitrate interest disputes is not needed in successive years; or rather, it is infrequently used.

Is there some loss of fiscal control? Yes. Is it, typically, of a significant magnitude? No.

Cases

Actual cases from real governmental units serve as excellent illustrations of the characteristics of dispute, arbitration, and resolution. Six public employment interest cases have been selected from the thousands of disputes which arise each year and result in impasse. Topically, the cases are different; several regions of the nation are represented. Some inter-occupational comparisons have been provided for, but four of the six cases involve certificated school personnel.

Board of Education, #26 and the Cary Education Association (IL, 1970)

In Cary, Illinois, a state with no public bargaining law, impasse occurred after the board voluntarily agreed to meet and confer with the local teachers' union. A panel of three heard the board and union presentations. For salaries, the comparability group selected by the teachers was composed of thirteen public schools in the area--high school, unified, and elementary school districts. The board's group included elementary districts only, on the basis of "purer" comparability. The teachers showed that the per pupil expenditures in Cary were the lowest among the eleven elementary districts in this grouping. The teachers compared median family income in the district to median teacher's salary; they compared past annual salary increases with increases in the cost of living. The board showed Cary as third from last among the seventeen elementary school districts of the county, on the basis of assessed valuation per pupil. The board proposed an across-the-board uniform raise, which worked out to a percentage raise of from 6. 6

to 3. 8%. The panel found the board's offer to be less than the cost-of-living increase for the year (5. 5%), declared the COL as minimum, and recommended a stable percentage. The panel proposed a new salary schedule in which every step would call for an increase of at least 5. 5%, and in which no step would yield more than 6. 6%. [8]

School District #29, North Merrick and the
Professional Association of Administrators (NY, 1970)

In New York the state public employment relations board (PERB) appointed an impartial fact-finder to assist in a board-administrator impasse. The issues were two: increasing the salary index for administrators which was attached to the teacher's base salary, and extending membership in the administrator's union to include non-certificated administrators. After hearings, the single arbiter, acting as a fact-finder, recommended: 1) that membership should not be increased, but implied that the non-certificated administrators could form their own group; 2) that the non-certificated administrators should get good dollar raises; 3) that the administrator's union should receive an index increase of . 03; e. g. , from 1. 35 to 1. 38 of the teacher's base for one class of administrators. [9]

City of Tulsa and Lodge 93, Fraternal Order of Police
(OK, 1973)

When the several aspects of compensation are lumped together, this case provides some insights into what is comparable. The Tulsa police union's proposal gave extensive attention to the city's ability to pay, having found a substantial cash reserve in the city's treasury. Median family incomes for various occupational groups in twenty-five selected cities were supplied. In a state with only one other comparable city, the comparative data had to be drawn from an out-of-state set of cities, developed through a rational selection procedure. The city provided data on manpower availability in the form of the excess of police applicants over job openings, almost 4:1. The city's set of comparable cities, selected on its own rational selection system, was eighteen. The neutral arbitrator considered the availability of money as a major item in his inclination toward a more, rather than a less, generous compensation award. [10]

Fairfax County (VA) and Fairfax County
Professional Firefighters Association, IAF #2068

Although this Virginia firefighters' dispute in 1972 included items other than salary, such as overtime and shift differentials, the approaches to the determination of salary were varied. In a year when the Bureau of Labor Statistics cost of living increase was 3.4%, the county board developed a pay increase proposal by multiplying 3.4 times the second step on the salary schedule. The product was $324 and that amount was offered as an across-the-board increase. The board concurrently proposed to reduce the number of years needed to reach the highest level on the salary schedule, and added some other compensation items. The union asked for 15%, and an impasse occurred. The arbiter's decision included the basic premise that all employees should get the COL as minimum. Noting a lag of almost one year in the COL data which had been used by the county, the decision was to bring the pay scale into time harmony with COL data. A raise of 6.3%, to include all compensation items--a total package--was awarded. [11]

Warren School Committee and Warren Education Association
(R. I., 1975)

A Rhode Island case was noteworthy for the unusually detailed aspects of the arbitrator's award, although some of those were only recommendations, not mandates. In addition to establishing base salary amounts, the award addressed the nine following conditions of employment:

1. No teacher should meet more than 170 pupils per day as an absolute maximum; when any load exceeds 125 pupils per day, load reduction should occur in other assignments.

2. Each teacher should have 225 minutes of un-assigned duty per week.

3. Every teacher should have a chair and lockable desk and file.

4. The definition of immediate family for death-in-the-family should be expanded to include brother or sister.

5. Teachers should be allowed three days with full

pay, chargeable to sick leave, for illness in the immediate household.

6. The union business days off with pay should be 20 days per year, less the costs of substitutes.

7. Teachers should be reimbursed for private car use at the rate of 15 cents per mile.

8. The board should seriously consider input from teachers as part of the administrator performance evaluation package.

9. Teachers should not be required to perform bus or playground duties; only when absolutely unavoidable, should teachers be required to assume duties in the cafeteria or at recess.

The detail and specificity was unusual. [12]

Fountain Valley School District and the FV Education Association (CA, 1975)

A 1975 California dispute ended with a fact-finder's recommendation that teachers should be granted an 8.5% salary increase for the 1975-76 school years. Some of the recommendations included statements about the generation of revenue (but those were highly specific to California's tax structure). Among the fact finder's additional recommendations were the following:

1. The board should grant to the union a reasonable amount of released time for union business.

2. The union should be allowed to use in-house communications patterns, without cost.

3. Teacher-administrator councils should be created with the goal of enhancing teacher involvement in the decision-making process.

4. Voluntary and involuntary transfers should be stabilized under a published procedure.

5. The grievance procedure should be extended one step to include advisory arbitration available to either teachers or board.

6. A management rights clause should be part of the contract.

7. The use of noon duty aides should be continued.

8. The insurance benefits portion of the fringe package should be continued. [13]

Calculating Settlements of Interest Disputes

Most disputes which occur during negotiations and which rise to impasse concern money. The disputes most frequently involve a salary offer from the employer which is less than the employee's demand. If that question goes to arbitration, how can an impartial panel, or a single arbiter, reasonably address the question?

One data source which has become important in salary settlements is the Consumer Price Index. The CPI, published by the Bureau of Labor Statistics, reveals a cost of living on certain common household expense categories in several regions of the United States. Many contracts have been negotiated recently in which the dollar amount becomes flexible after a period of time, and must be readjusted to harmonize with the cost of living (COL).

The CPI has been standardized on the basis of one dollar as equal to one dollar. Price changes in commodities and services are gathered monthly, and the general record since 1950 has been that the dollar has lost value, annually, as a purchasing unit. Quarterly reports reveal the change in each of the commodity categories for regions, and nationally. The CPI can be translated into percentages of increase or decrease. Percentages make the CPI a very usable and basic tool. With percentage calculations at hand for comparison purposes, it can be determined whether a salary offer is equal to the increase in the COL, and likewise, it can be seen to what degree a salary demand exceeds the COL. In Table 5.1, the year-end increases of the CPI have been translated into percentages and those increases are shown as annual and accumulative amounts.

To assure that readers use Table 5.1 appropriately, one example of its application is given here. Teachers are the most numerous category among public employees; combined with the long-existing single salary schedule, that

Table 5.1

Cost of Living Increases[14]

Starting years	50	66	67	68	69	70	71	72	73	74	75	1976
1976												5.8
75											9.1	15.4
74										11.0	21.1	28.1
73									6.2	17.9	28.7	36.1
72								3.3	9.7	21.8	32.9	40.6
71							4.3	7.7	14.4	27.0	38.6	46.6
70						5.9	10.5	14.1	21.2	34.5	46.8	55.3
69					5.4	11.6	16.4	20.2	27.7	41.7	54.7	63.6
68				4.2	9.8	16.3	21.3	25.3	33.1	47.7	61.2	70.5
67			2.9	7.2	13.0	19.7	24.8	28.9	36.9	52.0	65.8	75.4
66												
· · · ·												
50		34.8	38.7	44.5	52.3	61.3	68.2	73.8	84.6	104.9	123.6	136.5

category makes a good example over the twenty-five year span of the Table. In 1950, a typical base salary for teachers was about $3,000; in 1975, a typical base salary was about $8,000. Only a few calculations are needed to answer the question, did real purchasing power remain stable, go up, or go down?

(1)   8000 1975 salary   (2) $\frac{5000}{3000}$ = 1.67 x 100 = 167%
     -3000 1950 salary
      5000

(3)   167.0% earnings increase, 1950-75
     -136.5% COL increase, 1950-75
       30.5% net increase in purchasing power,
              1950-75

An arbitrator would very probably actually refine this formula. Statisticians would use a slightly different approach to the information in the table, but the result would not change substantially. The CPI is not, truly, an indicator of the COL because it omits some costs. In addition, federal and state income taxes are collected on the basis of a larger percentage for a larger gross income; i.e., the gain is never quite as much as it might first appear to be. Nevertheless, with all of the qualifications considered, in judging the effects of year-to-year salary disputes, Table 5.1 and the system of calculation combine into an adequate tool from which an arbiter can determine whether a salary offer is really a "break even" offer.

References

1. McDermott, Thomas. "Survey on Availability and Utilization of Arbitrators in 1972," in Barbara D. Dennis and Gerald G. Somers, eds., Arbitration of Interest Disputes. Proceedings of the 26th Annual Meeting, NAA. Washington: BNA Books, 1974, p. 261.

2. Statement by Earl E. Baderschneider, AAA publications associate editor. Personal interview, New York City, October 13, 1977.

3. Labor Arbitration in Government - 1344.

4. Fleming, R. W. "Interest Arbitration Revisited," in

Barbara D. Dennis and Gerald G. Somers, eds.,
Arbitration of Interest Disputes. Proceedings of
the 26th Annual Meeting, NAA. Washington: BNA
Books, 1974, pp. 1-7.

5. Berkowitz, Monroe. "Arbitration of Public Sector Interest Disputes: Economics, Politics, and Equity,"
in Barbara D. Dennis and Gerald G. Somers, eds.,
Arbitration--1976. Proceedings of the 29th Annual
Meeting of the NAA. Washington: BNA Books,
1976, p. 161.

6. Ibid., p. 166.

7. LAG - 686.

8. 12 - Arbitration in the Schools - 35.

9. 11 - AIS - 24.

10. LAG - 950.

11. LAG - 731.

12. 70 - AIS - 26.

13. 70 - AIS - 24.

14. Changing Times, November, 1977, p. 24-25.

Chapter 6

GRIEVANCES AND CONTRACT ARBITRATION

Introduction

     After a contract has been signed, sealed and de-
livered, disputes can, and do, still arise. Perfect working
settings are improbable. Unless intimidation, fear, resentment, or apathy prevail, disputes are inevitable and should
be expected. No contract means precisely the same thing
to all the parties to it. If left unresolved, grievable conditions become negative weights, bearing down upon employee
morale. Grievance procedures, established as routines
through which neutral third parties can function, are viable
and desirable parts of negotiated contracts.

     By prearrangement through the contract, a dispute,
i. e. , a grievance, can be referred voluntarily to an impartial third party for determination on the basis of evidence
and discussion. That prearrangement may also specify at
what level the arbiter's award will be accepted. That is,
will it be a recommendation, or will it be final and binding?
The contract may also stipulate the title under which the
neutral will work, and indicate whether the neutral shall be
an odd-numbered panel of, say, three or five persons, or a
single individual. The form or structure within which arbitration of a grievance occurs can be of several kinds. The
concept, however, is singular: grievances arising at the
work setting should come before a neutral outsider for a
hearing and resolution, when unresolved at a lower level
within the organization.

     What kinds of subjects have been grieved? For
teachers, arbitration has been used in a wide range of concerns, including sabbatical and personal leaves, promotion
and transfer, hours of work, duty-free lunch periods, time

for preparation, class schedules, and extracurricular assignments. It can be expected that several of these concerns will arise among other public employees, too.

Contract arbitration, the settlement of disputes arising during the life of a contract, is a low-profile settlement technique. It is designed to diminish hostilities and drain off antagonisms between the disputants, should there be any. Because it is a relatively new technique in the labor relations of public employment, and perhaps because many of the employing units are so small and intimate, the low-profile, diminished hostility concept is not so easily achieved as, historically, has been true in the private employment sector. The smaller the employing agency, the greater the danger that the mere filing of a grievance will be construed as an attack upon the personality or professional integrity of some of the persons involved. Of course, smaller agencies have frequently found that their short organization supervisory lines, coupled with personal familiarity, have been an adequate grievance resolution system. When difficulties quickly rise to the attention of a chief administrator, as should happen in smaller agencies, there is a decreased need for structured grievance techniques.

Grievances are filed to clarify issues. Prior to an arbitrator's decision, it cannot be known who is right and who is wrong on the arguable point. Occasionally, both parties have been found to be in the wrong, with the correct interpretation of the contract somewhere between.

Arbitration in collective negotiations, as between teachers and school administration, is a process whereby, if both parties fail to reach agreement, they may submit their dispute to a panel which recommends a course of action which is often a compromise; also called mediation, but often the mediator's findings are advisory rather than requiring compliance; if the parties are required to accept the decision, the process is called binding arbitration. [1]

Recourse to outside assistance is not an admission that contracts are disfunctional, or even fragile, but it is an acknowledgment of the inability of the negotiators to foresee all circumstances, and to write those circumstances lucidly precisely into the contract. The value of the contract, the labor agreement, is that by imposing a rule of law upon the work setting, it creates stability and reduces the number of instances which must be settled by temporary solutions-- which may have been developed suddenly and arbitrarily. [2] Given the facts of life about contracts, then, some form of arbitration (and that term construed very broadly) becomes an appropriate device to prevent the disintegration of the work setting.

Grievance Structures and Issues

Public agencies represent a wide range in mission. Even when a group of public agencies is reduced to a single category, range of mission prevails. In the nation there are about three thousand counties. By categorical name they are the same. However, their missions differ widely, partially because at different points in time different priorities arise and local preferences prevail. Those differences in priorities, and in size and finances, lead to necessary differentiation in employment practices. The same is true for public schools, hospitals, municipalities, and other agencies. There are, however, some features of the employee grievance structure which are fairly typical across the wide spectrum of public employment. Stated very briefly, a comprehensive provision for grievances would include the following four structures as in-house resolution devices.

> 1. Informal procedures: usually no more than a provision that the grievant and the supervisor attempt to resolve the problem before an appeal to a formal mechanism;

> 2. Written complaint: a provision that, when informal procedures have failed to resolve a conflict, the grievant will indicate in writing to an appropriate person or committee the nature of the complaint, the evidence on which it is based, and the redress sought;

> 3. Grievance Committee: this term ... refers to an individual, a committee, or a combination of the two, whose functions are to consider the written complaint and to resolve it or refer it to where it can be resolved;

> 4. Hearing Committee: this term refers to a committee especially established to consider a

particular case in which it is mandatory or desirable to provide for a quasi-judicial process, and where major policy issues or severe sanctions (e. g., dismissal) are involved. [3]

Each is a discrete structure, and the arrangement is from simplicity to complexity. Beyond the fourth structure would come an outside neutral party and "hired" arbitration.

The structures have been developed from experiences in labor relations, and they are designed to speak to issues. They provide direction and boundaries for consideration, forcing the issue toward resolution. For the structures to be most effective, impersonality must prevail along with a positive expectation; that same expectation must prevail when grievances escalate and demand the attention of an outside neutral.

Grievances must not be viewed with hostility by administrators. Unfortunately, given the perspective that the administrators of an organization are responsible for contract management, it is quite possible to hold the view that grievances arise from contract mismanagement. This is too simple a view. Boards or councils who hold their administrators responsible, in a negative sense, for grievances from the organization, have taken a too narrow view of their agencies. For grievance procedures to operate without hostility, it is imperative that grievances not be the occasion for evaluation of performance by any of the personnel who may be central to the dispute.

Openness, then, willingness, and receptivity must prevail within the ogranization. In that organizational environment, grievances can become a positive force within the agency because communications lines are opened. In a public school, for example, messages may flow freely between teachers, administrators, and board members. Policy statements or negotiated items which are weak may be exposed without risk, may be revised and strengthened, and future conflict reduced. The open, no-risk environment provides an opportunity for presenting and discussing the viewpoints of both parties; this in itself is a contribution to higher employee morale. Given a grievance procedure through either contract or statute, employees should

1. not hesitate to grieve real problems in the work setting;

2. not hunt for nor contrive grievable problems;

3. strive to settle the grievance quietly, quickly, and at the lowest administrative level possible.

Settlement, not spite, must be the goal. Grievances, like negotiations, must be carried forward in good faith.

Issues which are grievable are those in which there is the possibility of error in the organization's policies, in the procedures for carrying out those policies, in the administration of the procedures, or in varying combinations of the three situations. The same set of conditions which has been stipulated for policies pertain for negotiated items. Issues may arise from unilaterally developed items--policy--or from bilaterally developed items--written into the negotiated contract.

Typically, the issues have arisen from ".... the recruitment and selection of all employees, their assignment, working conditions, promotions, salaries, layoffs, terminations, retirement, and fringe benefits." All of those items have the potential to rise to the point of grievable issues; so do the grievance procedures themselves. [4]

In schools, formal grievance procedures for faculty have been used most heavily in four major issues: contract nonrenewal for probationary teachers, termination of teachers on tenure contracts, termination of contracts in mid-term, and disputed interpretations of entitlement to personal and medical leave. For noncertificated employees in schools, organizational grievance procedures have been less sharply focused, for these employees have been slow to unionize. Although some issues occur more frequently than others, there is virtually no limit upon the kind of dispute which may, if unresolved within the organization, demand the attention of an outside neutral as arbitrator.

Styles of Arbitration

Some contracts in private employment have been written with language that can best be described as open. Such contracts embody a recognition by the negotiators that a grievance arbitrator will be kept busy. Many large corporations hire full-time arbitrators who are, so to speak, in residence, the umpires for that locale. The only labor relations problems on which they work are those of the hiring corporation. Together, the arbiter and the negotiators form a complete labor relations team for that industry, and the satisfaction of both labor and management over extended periods of time attests to the suitability of the plan. Nothing quite like that exists in public employment.

For convenience of understanding, it should be helpful to think about three styles of public employment grievance arbitration: 1) narrow interpretation, 2) broad interpretation, and 3) flexible interpretation of the contract in applying it to grievance issues. Arbiters think and behave in discernible patterns; arbitral inclinations toward broad or narrow contract interpretations provide the evidence from which the patterns can be discerned when arbitration cases are read analytically. Some arbitrators have stated in a clear and unambiguous fashion the direction of their professional inclination; more often, it is implicit.

Each award in a grievance is a result of the application by the arbitrator of a set of decisional criteria. Some examples of broadly stated decisional rules which can be formed into selected stable decisional criteria are:

1. broaden and maintain the arbitrator's authority to determine the outcome;

2. harmonize arbitral authority within an existing framework of formal legal authority;

3. avoid conflict with other dispute settlement authorities by deferring decision-making authority to them;

4. consider only the words of the contract and principles related to contract law and rules of contract construction;

5. when faced with the question of whether law should be applied, apply only clearly applicable, unambiguous law or public policy;

6. it is the arbitrator's duty to interpret and then apply unclear law and public policy;

7. when law and the contract are in conflict, apply the contract command;

8. assess the effects of alternate, possible awards upon organizational efficiency, effectiveness, or morale;

9. apply whatever criteria the parties indicate that they desire. [5]

The application of the criteria to a specific dispute may be carried out narrowly, broadly, or flexibly. In the narrow view, which is sometimes labeled as the judicial style, grievance arbitration is seen as a system of private justice in which the contract is the source of both rights and duties. In this view, grievance arbitration is limited in time and scope by the specific stipulations of the contract. The contract is not construed as a general expression of the relationship between the two parties.

On the other hand, grievance arbitration may be viewed broadly in what is sometimes called the problem-solving style. Here, the contract is considered as indicative, but is recognized as not so extensive as to have provided for all contingencies in advance. Grievances not enumerated in the contract may be raised as issues nonetheless, because the contract is considered as a basic document, a product of the negotiations portion of the total collective bargaining endeavor. That document, the contract, may be extended through arbitration, which is another, naturally sequential part of that total collective bargaining endeavor. [6]

The two views, seen side by side in Table 6.1, can be appreciated as extreme positions. Neither is likely to exist in "pure" form. Some blending of the two views by the arbiter in pursuit of resolution produces that flexible position which is likely to be dictated by tests of common sense and reasonableness.

Grievance Procedures

The written agreements which become collectively negotiated contracts tend to become progressively longer. Accrual and extension occur through the years. The inclusion of grievance procedures in the written agreement is itself one such extender of the contract. Yet, such specificity is exactly what Justice Douglas was admiring in his comments on contract, because that specificity decreased the likelihood of interruptions in the public service. Simplicity and brevity

Table 6. 1

Arbitrator Styles[7]

Judicial Style	Problem-solving Style
Structure the proceeding as an adversarial contest in which professional advocates present arguments and proof to gain a decision in their clients' favor.	Take an active role in seeking information and raising points of discussion and argument.
Exclude matter which jeopardizes a fair proceeding or prejudices individual rights.	Observe organizational needs and imperatives (management and labor) prior to individual needs or "rights."
Use precedents in the writing of opinions and encourage its use by the parties.	Settle every dispute on the basis of its peculiar circumstances and equities without resort to precedents.
Define and sharpen the issue dividing the parties so as to permit a decision to be made between competing claims.	Seek reduction of conflict in an effort to effect cooperation and a state of joint bargaining between the parties.
Use formal rules to regularize the hearing and to preclude consideration of irrelevant material.	Use informality and be tolerant of irrelevant material.
Insist upon making the record of the open hearing the sole factual basis for decision in the case.	Consider any relevant information regardless of whether introduced in the hearing or obtained outside of it.

are to be admired, too, but not when quality of the contract must be sacrificed to achieve them. A good example of a comprehensive statement on grievances is in the contract between the Lincoln Education Association and the Lincoln, Nebraska Board of Education.[8] It will be examined in depth.

In an opening statement of purpose and intent, the

employers and employees join to laud good morale as an enhancement to job performance. A grievance is defined as follows:

> Grievance shall mean a claim by one or more employees of a violation, a misapplication or misinterpretation of the state statutes, board policies, administrative directives or regulations under which such employees work, specifying that which is claimed to be violated and the specifics of such violation. The term "grievance" shall not apply to any matter for which (1) the method of review is prescribed by law, or (2) the Board of Education is without authority to act.
>
> Should a teacher have a claim based upon an event or condition which affects the teacher's welfare or morale, but may not be processed under the above definition, the teacher shall have the right to use normal administrative channels to solve the problem. This process shall commence with a conference with the teacher's immediate supervisor.

Ten general conditions under which the procedure operates are itemized. The first condition, compliance, has proved to be troublesome in all work settings. Compliance is a demand put upon the employee. That is, even when directives are thought to be in conflict with policy or contract, the employee must follow the directive. (When an employee receives a directive which appears to be wrong, it is difficult professionally to follow it; but to refuse a directive, either oral or written, would place the employee in a condition of insubordination. Generally, insubordination is sufficient basis for dismissal.) The employee must comply, but compliance does not necessarily indicate acceptance or approval, and does not prejudice the employee's rights to grieve the directive, nor "... shall it affect the ultimate resolution of the grievance." Other conditions of the grievance are:

1. no reprisals
2. time limitations, gradated by the levels or steps in the grievance sequence
3. provisions for failure to meet time limitations, by labor or management
4. communications in writing
5. no adjustment of grievances; each stands as it occurred
6. forms for processing

7. meetings for hearings
8. no interference with the work of the school
9. representation assistance for the employee allowed as stipulated.

With a complete set of definitions and each successive step in the procedure clearly delineated, the contractual routine has been designed to defuse much of the hostility which sometimes surrounds grievances. For employees who exhaust the four-step in-house resolution routine, and who are yet dissatisfied, there still exists a recourse outside of the school. Arbitration assistance may be sought. In Nebraska, with its unique Court of Industrial Relations acting as the arbiter, a few cases of individual grievances have been heard. None have come from Lincoln. In the 1970s the few cases have come from public schools and municipalities. In any other state, a more common form of arbitration would probably be used.

Cases

From among the thousands of grievances which rise to arbitration annually, seven have been selected, all of which have occurred in the past few years. Many of the most common characteristics of grievance disputes can be seen in these cases. The issues include personnel evaluation, insubordination, length of the workday, and pupil teacher ratios. Several states are represented in the seven cases, and some inter-occupational comparisons have been provided.

Arlington Education Association and
Arlington Board of Education (VA, 1971)

In 1971 in Arlington, Virginia, a teacher sought and obtained a maternity leave--but it was given with the condition of uncertainty of re-employment. An arbiter from the AAA served as the neutral to hear each side present interpretations of the pertinent contract clause(s). The association contended that the administration had reverted to a board policy which preceded the negotiated contract, but that the contract was the current governing document. The administration spoke of the need to protect flexibility in manpower planning. The arbitrator found that a teacher on maternity leave should have the same status with regard to re-employment as another teacher not on maternity leave, and that the school district lacked a contractual base to condition a pregnant teacher's return from leave. [9]

Carroll County Board of Education and Carroll County Education Association (MD, 1975)

An arbitrator was assigned by the AAA to handle a grievance from a Maryland teacher who had been evaluated downward on the basis of refusing to participate in extracurricular activities when asked to do so by a principal. The contract stipulated that teachers had an option, to participate or not, and also stipulated that tenured teachers would be evaluated annually. This tenured teacher opted not to participate, but did not want to be evaluated down for that choice. The arbiter pointed out that the contract clause had been negotiated and signed by both parties. The right to abstain from such a duty assignment was clear. Evaluation, used for coercion, would be an erosion of contract rights. The award was in favor of the grievant. [10]

Akron City Hospital and AFSCME Local 684 (OH, 1976)

A case which involved insubordination arose in Akron when a surgical room orderly was dismissed. At the time of hiring, the orderly was given a job description which was thoroughly explained. He was to take orders from nurses, not doctors. However, doctors were quite willing to give him orders, and did, and he sometimes accepted them if no nurses were present. Occasionally, this made him unavailable to a nurse in need of his assistance. On such occasions, he was reprimanded orally. The final violative act came when a nurse "caught" him suturing a patient. The presiding doctor had invited him to do so, and he had done sutures previously in the hospital's surgical rooms. He was dismissed as an insubordinate on the basis that he placed the hospital in jeopardy for malpractice. Acknowledging that the orderly had worked beyond his job description, the arbiter also pointed out that the grievant could not have been insubordinate because he had never been told directly by a supervisor not to suture. The discharge was set aside as lacking just cause, and the grievant reinstated with back pay and one week's suspension. [11]

Community Unit School District and the
Unit Education Association (IL, 1976)

The question to be resolved in this Illinois school centered about the length of the school day. Board policy, which was not new, stipulated that a school day would "... normally be from 8 a. m. to 4 p. m." A negotiated contract clause of a later date stipulated that "... the teacher's professional day shall consist of the time necessary for the teacher to complete his/her professional duties." Then, the Board attempted to reinstate the clock times of its own policy statement. The arbiter found no state laws barring the Board from delegating judgment on the day length to the teachers through the contract. Witnesses provided no evidence of abuse of that delegation. The award was in favor of the union on the premise that teachers were adequate judges of their professional duties. 12

Madison Board of Education # 8 and
Madison Teachers Inc. (WI, 1975)

Extra duty assignments are frequently a problem. A Wisconsin principal had assigned bus-loading supervision duty to teachers for several years. In all other schools of the district this work was performed by principals or bus supervisors. The existing contract stipulated that any changes in the terms and conditions of teachers' employment must be negotiated. The board pointed out that the contract did not forbid or preclude such assignments, and that the management rights clause provided the authority for such assignments. The arbiter held that bus loading was not in the "field of instruction," and was, therefore, outside the management rights clause and must be negotiated. It was directed that the negotiation include compensation for bus-loading service performed after the date of the grievance, but that no consideration be given any work done prior to the filing of the grievance. The arbiter also commented that "Teachers may volunteer for such service and be compensated" after the parties have negotiated the rate. 13

Woonsocket School Committee and
Woonsocket Teachers Guild (R. I., 1975)

In Rhode Island a contract stipulated that class size would not exceed 25 pupils, except for specific reasons enumerated in the contract. The administration scheduled primary classes of from 29 to 32 pupils, and the circumstance was grieved. One of the exceptions under which classes could exceed 25 pupils was shortage of spaces, and it was contended that it was precisely the space problems which led to the larger classes. An inventory of space in district buildings revealed that classrooms were available in schools, one as near as two miles from the school where the grievance arose. The administration declared it had acted in good faith because when a similar grievance had previously arisen, the award had been in favor of the board. However, this arbiter declared that previous decision as having no bearing, and held that the board was in violation of the agreement. It was pointed out that before the claim of inadequate space could stand, the board would have to act to remedy the problem in some way other than contract violation, e. g. , transportation of pupils or shifting building attendance lines. [14]

Norton School Committee and
Norton Teachers Association (MS, 1976)

The manner in which personal leave may be taken varies with the stipulations of the contract. In this Massachusetts school, the contract stipulated that teachers could take personal leave "... for the purpose of attending to personal matters that cannot be reasonably attended to outside of the normal workday. " The board required teachers seeking personal leave to include the reasons for the leave on the request form, and that requirement was grieved. Through negotiations, the board had accomplished a restriction on personal leave, and the explicitly stated reasons for the leave provided the only basis from which the board could determine whether or not the matter could be attended to outside of the normal workday. Earlier contracts had not called for any reason to be given, but at the same time that the board agreed to a carryover of unused personal leave days, it secured a condition upon their use. The award was a denial of the grievance as the arbiter ruled that applying teachers had to state reasons for the requested leave. [15]

Norfolk Board of Education and
Norfolk Education Association (CN, 1976)

Discharge is an extreme disciplinary measure. A

Connecticut teacher grieved her firing over a matter of personal leave. She had a reputation as a competent and dedicated teacher. She requested personal leave to accompany her husband on vacation. It was denied, but she went anyway, acting in contradiction to a direct order. The board dismissed her. The state allowed but did not mandate dismissal of a teacher for insubordination. The grievant had requested two days of paid leave at the beginning of the school year. During her absence, a qualified substitute replaced her and followed lesson plans which she had prepared. Upon return she was notified of termination for insubordination. The award stipulated that she should be reinstated, that a letter of reprimand should go into her personnel folder, and that she should suffer a five-day suspension without pay. [16]

Individual Rights and Collective Bargaining

Grievances have often developed from instances in which individual employees have felt wronged. Class actions have come, too, but individual workers have discovered, in the contract developed through negotiations, a strong protection of many of their rights, as these are specified and enumerated in the contract. The contract is a unique document, a privately, bilaterally developed document which, in essence, represents government by the consent of the governed while at work. Public employees, working for a governmental subdivision, become parties to a private contract, in precise parallel to private employees. The fact that the contract is collective in coverage does not detract from its privacy; like the simplest contract between individuals, it is a private agreement.

That essence of privacy was extended in contract administration, which included arbitration of grievances. In fact, commencing with World War II, the success of bargaining, augmented by arbitration, reduced greatly the incidence of disruption of production. The efficacy of collective bargaining and arbitration in labor relations was obvious, and was endorsed by the few court appeals which arose, notably in the trilogy decisions of 1960. The sanctity of the private agreement, privately developed and administered, prevailed as a corollary to judicial restraint.

The 1960s and '70s saw a voluminous growth of statutes, rulings, and regulations aimed at preserving individual rights. Government, demonstrating its power, spoke to the

terms and conditions of employment, addressing worker
health and safety, pensions, equal pay, and other matters.
The recognition of and incorporation of publicly conferred
individual rights into collectively bargained contracts became
a problem. Contracts were never intentionally developed upon
unlawful bases; but a new level of publicly imposed complexity now had to be accommodated. Moreover, without any attempt to identify or separate as cause or effect, it can be
observed that, concurrently, the judicial restraint of the
early 1960s vanished. Courts stood ready to hear appeals
from rulings by arbitrators. The private world of the private contract, privately administered and adjudicated, disappeared, and its disappearance was not upon any planned
basis.

Arbitration, like every other human endeavor, is performed at different quality levels. Some of the case sum-
maries presented earlier hint at discrepancies in arbitral
decisional quality. Some judges openly attacked arbitral ineptness, alleging partiality and incompetence as further rationale for judicial review of decisions by arbitrators. Others,
through their decisions, implied certain inadequacies by arbiters. For many reasons, then, it is now becoming quite
clear that the judiciary branch of government, seeing itself
as socially active in the broadest sense, is becoming an increasingly influential force in labor relations. The implications for cost escalation and time extension are huge. As
a practical recognition of this circumstance, a proposal for
"workable coordination" has been set forward. Arbitrators
must recognize the strong possibility of judicial review of
their awards. At the same time, the court must acknowledge
the public importance of the likelihood of finality in arbitration decisions. Stability in labor relations and trust in the
contract as a document for the protection of individual rights
demands judicial restraint and discrete implementation of
the review function: "... then [we will] obtain the requisite
measure of predictability as to the firmness of results coming
out of the arbitral sphere, ... if effective collective bargaining is still to be considered a cherished national goal."[17]

References

1. Good, Carter V. , ed. Dictionary of Education. 3rd ed.
   Englewood Cliffs, N. J. : Prentice-Hall, 1973.

2. United Steelworkers v. Warrior & Gulf Navigation Co.,
   363 U. S. 574 (1960).

3. Furniss, W. Todd. Grievance Procedure: A Working Paper. Washington, D. C.: American Council on Education, 1975, p. 2.

4. Ibid., p. 5.

5. Pops, Gerald, Emergence of the Public Sector Arbitrator. Lexington, Mass.: Lexington Books, D. C. Heath and Co., 1976, p. 84. Reprinted by permission of the publisher. Copyright 1976, D. C. Heath and Company.

6. Ibid., p. 31.

7. Ibid., pp. 84-85.

8. Lincoln Education Association and Board of Education. Negotiated Settlement. Lincoln, NE: Lincoln Public Schools, May, 1974.

9. 27 - Arbitration in the Schools - 10

10. 62 - AIS - 2

11. Labor Arbitration in Government - 1763

12. 79 - AIS - 2

13. 74 - AIS - 11

14. 74 - AIS - 11

15. 75 - AIS - 21

16. 75 - AIS - 10

17. Valtin, Rolf. "The Presidential Address: Judicial Review Revisited--The Search for Accommodation Must Continue," in Barbara D. Dennis and Gerald G. Somers, eds., Arbitration--1976. Proceedings of the 29th Annual Meeting of the NAA. Washington: BNA Books, 1976, p. 11.

Chapter 7

STRIKES

Introduction

Any enterprise or organization may cease to function for some cause. In the labor-management milieu, organizations may halt the delivery of a product or service for several reasons. In private enterprise, one method by which the organizations may be halted is the lock-out. During the lock-out, workers are not allowed to enter the place of employment. Lock-outs do not occur in public employment because governing boards have performance mandated to them. For example, a city council may not lock-out the firefighters even though there may be a dispute with little hope of resolution in the foreseeable future. Likewise, a board of education may not lock-out the teachers. Public governing boards have performance obligations which are set forward in statutes or ordinances. The lock-out is one method of extreme impact which private management possesses and may use in labor relations, but which public management does not possess.

Another pressure technique of extreme impact is the strike. The strike is available to labor but unavailable to management. Although the term work-stoppage may be awkward, it is also descriptive. It describes the strike. Comparable to the strike, but more restricted in its impact, are sanctions. Sanctions have had rather widespread use over several decades and in restricted occupational categories; currently, sanctions are not much in use. The two techniques, strike and sanction, represent the ultimate in employee militancy, short of violence.

Most of the collective bargaining laws which apply to public employees have had such stated intentions as the improvement of personnel management, enhancement of the quality of service being provided by the affected occupational categories, and the promotion of personal welfare of the employees. Most employee groups have lobbied long and loudly to secure for themselves the right of affiliation into an organization of their choice, and to use it as the vehicle for employment relations with public governing boards. The collective bargaining statutes have been aimed, then, more at the employees and less at the employers, in the sense that the statutes confer rights.

The laws have been modeled after the private employment sector of the world of work. It has been assumed that what has served employees well in one setting could be transferred to another setting and still work well. Some problems must be candidly recognized, however. Production is more difficult to define precisely when service, rather than some tangible product, is the reason for the organization. Most public employees deliver a service. It is a problem to identify the consumer of a service; it may be several persons, and some of the consumption may be indirect. It is a problem to determine equity of service cost, given the fact that many of the services are provided in non-competitive settings; e. g. , the consumer could not choose an alternative public service, even if he wanted to, in regard to schools, police and fire protection, and so on. Many other problems could be listed, but it is sufficient to note again that the private and public sectors of the economy are not perfectly parallel.

The quality level at which an organization performs is a central concern in both the private and public sectors. When performance deteriorates, the consumer is adversely affected. That is true, for example, in education. There, it may be rather difficult to identify the consumer, unless it is arbitrarily agreed that students are the consumers of education. The arbitrariness of such a decision rests upon the fact that the community, generally, might also be logically identified as the consumer of education. But whether agreement on consumer identification is reached or not, when services falter, when quality falls, reaction sets in. Inefficient management may adversely affect quality. So may unreasonable labor demands. In the delivery of a service at some cost by any public agency, it might be said that maximum deterioration is a work-stoppage. In fact, in that condition, the service has not only deteriorated; it has disappeared. [1]

Work-stoppages have been used in the private sector

as an economic lever. In the public sector, on whatever base they may be proposed, work-stoppages have occurred under several names. Sometimes, the workers have labeled them as vacation days, illness days, or invented some other disguise of reality, while keeping the label consistent with their particular setting. In education, there was a time when sanctions were applied against local school boards or states, but not under the label of sanctions. Now, work-stoppages are called more candidly what they really are; i. e., strikes. Honest use of terminology seems to have "set in, " and some of this candor can be attributed to job security which is union related.

In dealing with topics that are socially important and which have both proponents and opponents, the question of advocacy arises. Advocacy of collective bargaining is the position of this text. That advocacy rests upon the belief that there are constructive elements in society with a "natural bent" toward goal achievement, that society is reasonably systematic and that humanity is not in wild pursuit of chaos. The strike as one powerful tool in bargaining settings is not advocated, nor is there advocacy for its withdrawal from the public employment sector. That question deserves attention, but that is not the purpose of this book. Advocacy of the process of collective bargaining is a testimony of faith in communications which, when carried out in an atmosphere of equality and good faith, can contribute to mutually acceptable conditions of work and employment, to compensation and per- formance. Compared to unilaterally determined contracts, collective bargaining is much more complex, but its lack of simplicity does not mean that it is less effective. After all, incentives are determiners of what people do--and how well they do it--and participation in the identification of incentives carries its own value. Here, complexity appears to influence work performance positively.

The irreconcilable impasse which may lead a union into such extreme action as sanction or strike may well hinge upon disputes over what is negotiable. The union may insist that an item is within the scope of bargaining, and the public board may assert that to bargain on the item would be an unlawful delegation of power. The scope itself may be variable over the large range of public employees, lead- ing to misunderstandings or to willingness to test the law. For instance, state employees in Vermont have much more latitude in choice of bargainable items than do firemen, who are municipal employees in the same state. Confusion and dispute over scope, then, may lead to strikes. [2]

Standard data developed to keep track of strike activity showed it to be in decline in the early seventies. The decline, for all organized workers, was more noticeable for private than for public employees (see Figure 7. 1). In 1970, there were over 5, 600 work stoppages.

Figure 7. 1

Strike Activity[3]

Number work days
lost to work
stoppages

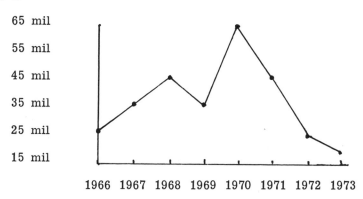

65 mil

55 mil

45 mil

35 mil

25 mil

15 mil

1966 1967 1968 1969 1970 1971 1972 1973

Sanctions

Because sanctions have great flexibility and because their use may be fashioned so that their presence is only as apparent as the involved employees desire, sanctions as a work-stoppage method will be discussed before strikes. Sanctions were developed by the National Education Association as an alternative to strikes. Sanctions consist of pressures exerted by the organized workers against employing boards, or even against entire states. Statewide sanctions have been applied in Florida, Oklahoma, and other places. The sanctions come in the form of gradated and sequential levels of impact, and they are:

> 1. An advisory, issued to members, warning them of unsatisfactory working conditions under a specific public board.

2. A request to members that they not seek employment from the offending board.

3. A request to currently employed members that they seek employment elsewhere, or in another field.

4. A statement to union members that they should refrain from employment by that offending board, coupled with the threat of expulsion from the union if they accept or continue employment.

T. M. Stinnett, speaking for the National Education Association in the mid-sixties, described sanctions as follows:

Sanctions do not violate a contract. Services to children are not interrupted. There are no picket lines. School districts are given several months' notice and told that existing conditions make possible only inferior programs for children; that professional people cannot, under the existing conditions, provide first-rate services. [4]

Much, much more than any other public employee group, teachers have used sanctions. They did so because, for most of the sixties, it was important to teachers to identify their bargaining activity as different from the bargaining activity of labor, where that activity had historically unfolded. That is, teachers saw themselves as professionals, and therefore apart from, for example, municipal sanitation workers who might have membership in some "mainline" labor union. It was important to this group of well over one million workers--the teachers--to maintain distance between themselves and labor. Too, sanctions had not been newly invented in the NEA.

In education, sanctions had been available at least since 1917. The NEA's Code of Ethics, adopted in 1929, stated that teachers must "refuse to accept a position when the vacancy had been created through unprofessional activity or pending controversy over professional policy or the application of unjust personnel practices and procedures." [5] Little use was made of this by teachers.

Apparently, prior to 1951, teacher sanctions were applied in fewer than a dozen cases. In three cases which occurred in the states of Ohio, Montana and Washington, the problems which led to sanctions were resolved, and in each case, the resolution was "in favor" of the teachers' group applying the sanctions.

By 1962, the NEA had once again begun officially to mention professional negotiations. The Association adopted a sterner resolution concerning negotiations. It stressed the importance of boards recognizing the rights of teachers to meet with them as equal partners in determining policies which were stipulated as being of mutual concern. Emphasis was still placed on both parties recalling that they were public bodies and not resorting to the dispute settlement techniques which prevailed in industry. Teachers were "professional" and should not resort to strikes; this was the "line" coming from the NEA while the AFT in the New York City Schools was striking and getting good settlements.

Out of the 1962 NEA Convention came a resolution entitled "Professional Sanctions." It stated that:

> The National Education Association believes that, as a means of preventing unethical or arbitrary policies or practices that have a deleterious effect on the welfare of the schools, professional sanctions should be invoked. These sanctions would provide for appropriate disciplinary action by the organized profession.
> The National Education Association calls upon its affiliated state associations to co-operate in developing guidelines which define, organize, and definitely specify procedural steps for invoking sanctions by the teaching profession. 6

This marked the beginning of the official adoption of a pressure tactic by the NEA, but it stopped short of anything which it might be labeled as a strike.

One major case provided a new understanding of the legality of sanctions. In the Board of Education, Borough of Union Beach v. New Jersey Education Association (1967), an extended commentary was provided by the Superior Court of New Jersey.

The defendant New Jersey Education Association, with a membership of about 57,000, and its local affiliate established a list of seventeen grievances against the local board. The central item of dispute was the board's decision not to re-employ a probationary teacher. The leverage aspect of the sanctions was manifested in mass resignations by the local teachers and a "blacklisting" of the local school district throughout the state by the state education association. The goal was to bring to a halt the function of that local government agency; that is, to close the schools, or to force the local board of education to change its positions.

The court took note of the terminology under which the action occurred, then commented that the substance of a situation must be the controlling factor in describing that situation, and not the terms insistently applied by the departed teachers. The sequence of events staged by the teachers' union led the court to note the presumptiousness of that private group, and to find against the local and state associations because the work-stoppage was a strike in fact, if not in name. With strikes prohibited by state statute, an injunction was issued, ordering the "striking" teachers back to work.

Except as they may be subtly applied, sanctions have fallen from favor within the only occupational category which ever gave sanctions a strong place in the public labor relations picture.

Strikes

A strike is not the action of a single employee; employees combine to withdraw their labor at some pre-arranged time for the purpose of securing an advantage to themselves. A strike is a work-stoppage; that is, the regularly scheduled activities of the organization are interrupted. Generally, a strike can be viewed as a temporary stoppage, carried out by employees who are using it as a technique to bring about compliance with demands being made upon an employer. Examples of such demands would be to achieve higher wages, shorter hours, or better working conditions. The essence of the strike is coercion.

Sometimes, strikes are less than the withdrawal of workers from their place. Sit-down strikes have occurred. The "slow-down" is a kind of interruption which has application in private enterprise settings where a product is the outcome. That technique would have obvious application in factory assembly line settings, but it can also be used by public employees in the delivery of services which have any kind of time sequence in the delivery. In many public employment settings, though, the application of a "slow-down" would not be readily apparent. Practically, the strike, when used by public employees, means a work-stoppage, and it must have an effect.

The private sector collective bargaining model assumes a market place constraint upon both employers and employees in the decision to buy or not to buy the produce or the service, whichever is being marketed, and the price of which may be affected by the settlement of the strike. Two factors operate to make this model less viable in the public sector: 1) the monopolistic characteristic of public boards charged to deliver a product or service; 2) the separation of tax collection from the delivery of that product or service, obscuring the connection in the mind of the consumer. The companion assumptions in the private sector, such as loss of profits and wages, affect the public sector less, if at all. The models are not perfectly interchangeable, but the lineage of public sector strikes is apparent, and those events had their origin in the private sector. [7]

Historical Development of the Strike

It is surely appropriate to comment that discontent with the status quo is the prime mover of economic and social change. With the emergence of the wage-earning class, groups with different goals and tendencies have claimed the right to exploit that discontent and to convert it into a vehicle for some sort of change. "Labor unrest is commonly centered on specific grievances, which have to be remedied after a fashion if any organization is to become the chosen instrument." The worker discontent can be turned in more than one direction, and used for more than one purpose. [8] The strike is one tool which may serve some of those purposes. It must be emphasized that the goal of a strike is not to break the organization; it is only intended to be a temporary withholding of function.

Some of the earliest strikes in England and the United States were quite similar to present-day industrial conflicts. That is, they were sponsored by continuing labor organizations, they had well defined objectives, and they showed evidence of carefully formulated strategy. Many, perhaps most, had a different character, however. "Rather than organized, they were unorganized; or to be more accurate the striking workers were thrown together into an ad hoc organization, with or without a name, which often disappeared when the strike had ended. "[9] Rather than being calculated, they were impulsive; and although based on deeply felt grievances, they were not marked by clear notions of how the grievances were to be remedied, or how the remedies were to be obtained and implemented. Many of the early strikes among skilled workers were spontaneous eruptions of workers at the end of their patience. "The incidence of violence in the early strikes was inversely proportioned to the degree of the organization. "[10] Those characteristics prevailed in the railroad strike which began in July, 1877 at Martinsburg, West Virginia. Incited by a ten per cent pay cut which came upon the heels of an earlier pay cut, the railroaders gathered and halted the movement of the trains. That strike featured anger, violence, fatalities, military intervention, and no clear-cut goals for which the workers were striving. [11]

There is evidence that the strong proprietorship which trade-unions presently exercise over the strike in the United States was not achieved until after World War I, and that more than one-third of all strikes were unorganized as late as the beginning of this century. During many of the years between 1880 and 1900 the number of workers involved in strikes was greater than the number of union workers, indicating that many workers joined in sympathy at critical times. Much of this unrest could be attributed to job drudgery, a characteristic of the narrow and monotonous tasks accompanying industrialization. Charles P. Neill, Commissioner of Labor, made some positive remarks about the latter in his annual report of 1910. He commented on the need to recognize this burdensome condition, and detailed the manner in which states were establishing methods and institutions for industrial education. Typically, those industrial education efforts were being mounted by public school systems to upgrade and improve the oversupply of unskilled and low-grade labor. [12] Speaking directly to problems of job satisfaction, such efforts must have had a controlling effect on strikes and lost man-days.

Nineteenth-century unions, such as the Grand National Consolidated Trades Union and (later) the Knights of Labor, wanted to accomplish gains for worker-members. Generally, that was their offering to prospective members. However, in the governmental climate of that day, strikes were so unpopular that to attempt them usually led to disaster; to attempt to lead labor without their use also led to disaster.

Perhaps it was less the technique and more the tenor of the times, in which all or most labor activity was suspect; the fact is, however, that strikes as a tool of labor did not flourish in the U. S. during the nineteenth century--and that is a great understatement!

In the twentieth century, a different attitude came to prevail, but only gradually. Union leaders recognize that it is good business practice, that it establishes honesty and credibility, to discipline their unions, disallowing strikes during times when a contract is in operation. When the strike occurs, one goal is to minimize damage to the industry and loss of supportive public opinion. That experienced union leader sentiment translates readily into the public sector in such a setting as a county or municipal hospital struck by physicians or nurses, but continuing operation by way of "emergency staffing. " In life or death situations, public opinion will quickly turn against the strikers if all services are completely denied--and public opinion is important to any union.

Wildcat strikes occur outside the jurisdiction of union leaders, and perhaps against their advice, and can damage the union internally and result in loss of public prestige for the union. Despite such considerations, wildcat strikes--undisciplined work-stoppages during the term of a contract--do occasionally occur.

At a glance, it may appear that in those strikes which occur during the term of a contract, management is utterly helpless. Such is not the case. A union may not breach a contract with impunity. If management wants to take some action of such severity that it will influence future considerations in which a union may engage prior to a decision to strike, it may choose from several alternatives. For example, when New York City's United Federation of Teachers went on strike in October, 1976, at a time when it had a contract in force, the schools sought and obtained a penalty ruling from the state's Public Employment Relations Board. The PERB relieved the school board of its contractual obligation to provide for the union the automatic payroll deduction of dues, which was a part of the breached contract. That five-day walkout was also ruled as in violation of New York's Taylor Law of 1967, which prohibits strikes by public employees. Although not a wildcat strike, this work-stoppage was comparable in that it occurred while a valid contract was in force, and in this instance the governing board chose to hit at the union's pocketbook as a penalty.

The outcome is still unsettled, for the UFT is seeking an injunction against the PERB ruling, and an order for reinstatement of the dues check-off system. The union's suit includes other interests, too. If the PERB decision stands, past experience indicates that the union would stand to lose about $50,000 per month in lost dues which will not be paid by teacher members if not collected in payroll deduction. Continued over many months, revenue loss would be substantial, even for such a large union as the UFT in New York, and the event stands as a good example of a tool which management possesses to combat strikes by public employees while they have a contract in force.

Strikes in the Public Sector

As an occupational type, teachers provide a good case study of worker viewpoints toward strikes in that, comparatively, they are at about a midpoint in professionalization. That is, to the extent that professionalization can be connected to academic accomplishment, teachers are somewhere between physicians who might strike against a public hospital, and firefighters who might strike against a county or municipality. There are ambiguities which confuse the comparative status picture for teachers, and one such factor is the characteristic that they are employees, and not fee takers. Some categorizations eliminate employees from any professional group. That is not the point of this comparison; in fact, it is not material. The midpoint illustration should still stand.

Some recent studies, which have attempted to determine reasons why teachers strike, have not had perfect congruence. Some findings have indicated that economic reasons lead all others; yet there are other studies indicating that the strike propensity among teachers is most often occasioned by their desire for more control over their work setting.

Teacher militancy, and the degree to which it is exhibited, is an indicator of propensity to strike. Teacher militancy is also a protective device, maintained as a front against student protests, demands by parents for control over schools, demands by civil rights advocates, and taxpayer revolts. Being, in a sense, the target for all such groups, teachers have become militant in their own quest for authority. Presently, militancy is still a small part of the average teacher's attitude structure; that is, it is not a real factor in teachers' associations activities to influence educational policy. Among teacher unions, the New York UFT's history identifies it as comparatively militant. Its stand against decentralization and community control must have been viewed by civil rights groups as conservative and reactionary, positions not characteristically ascribed to unions, and particularly "young" unions. [13]

In a broader setting, student demands have been viewed by teachers over the nation very pragmatically. When students gain power, who loses it? Teachers see themselves as the group giving up power in that transfer. Part of teacher reluctance in this setting is professionally based, but much of that attitude is generated out of concern for personal welfare, too. Militance by individuals and union strength are joined as one manifestation of teacher hostility toward many demands by students. Militant teachers, a very small minority, are generally well respected in the larger teacher group. When, in their judgment, situations arise which call for resistance or action, another larger, and typically silent group, materializes and will come to their support. Among their peers, militants are a small, strategically located, and prestigious group. Their origin, sex, and teaching assignment may vary, but social science teachers are disproportionately represented. Every teacher is aware of the power transfer from teachers to students which has been a part of the civil rights action of the past decade or so. All, then, are potential supporters for that very small, energetic group which may take up the cudgel, and teachers see bargaining settings as one place where some power over their working conditions may be regained or reasserted.

Militancy may be developmental or reactionary. Its presence may be generated by working conditions or by economic drives. It is a matter of degree, but it is surely fair to state that strikes by public employees would rarely occur, given the absence of militance.

The willingness of teachers to strike is new to the labor scene. Teachers have not viewed the strike as a very promising endeavor; yet the incidence of teacher strikes and the number of instructional days "lost" has increased through the sixties and into the early seventies, suggesting an altered viewpoint. This change has also been borne out by inquiring research among teachers. With teaching personnel surpluses now occurring, and likely to extend through the next several years, it becomes difficult to predict what teachers will do and what their attitudes will be, through the latter seventies and into the eighties, as they consider the question, "Shall we strike?"

Any strike must have as one consideration its acceptance by the affected publics. Will the public become hostile toward the striking groups? Repeatedly, research among population groups has revealed that the general public is more tolerant to the idea of teacher strikes, school boards are less tolerant, and school administrators not tolerant at all. It is the latter group which sees the management-labor relationship close-up, and from a biased point of view. Acceptability of teacher strikes is related to location, too. Small, homogeneous communities have little tolerance for the idea; large, heterogeneous communities provide a comparatively tolerant environment. [14]

Many factors bearing upon the likelihood of strikes are closely related to the critical question, "Who is in charge?" That central question reduces to specifics for the governing boards of counties, cities, school districts, and other agencies. "Should teachers set policy for the schools? Should social workers help set welfare standards? Should policemen have a voice in determining the size and deployment of the police force?" After spending the initial years of collective bargaining in an intensive pursuit of salary improvement, public employees are attempting to broaden the scope of negotiations. The American Federation of State, County and Municipal Employees has articulated that extended concern, noting that for such professionals as the teacher or the case worker, "... things like class size and case load become as important as the hours in a shift is to the blue-collar worker." Wages have been improved; hours and working conditions are becoming the focal points. [15]

Some specifics about teacher strikes are instructive. In the Fall of 1977, the NEA identified sixty-two walkouts, a smaller number than occurred in the Fall of 1976. The most frequently mentioned causes of 1977 strikes were disputes in four areas:

1. class size control,
2. reduction in force contract provisions,
3. salary and fringe benefits,
4. discipline. [16]

Another perspective can be gained from a closer

examination of one of those strikes, the four-week strike by 1,600 teachers in Yonkers, N. Y. Walking out on September 7, the teachers wanted new guarantees on job security and salary increases. In settlement, the teachers got a two-year contract which provided a 13.2 per cent wage increase over the two years, with 9.2 per cent of that coming in the first year. Although the school district had attempted to provide partial instructional services to its pupils, the "half measures" had not been popular in the district and more than half of the 26,000 pupils did not attend. Some parents sued the board, demanding the development of an escrow fund which would support tuition claims as children were enrolled in neighboring public schools or nearby private schools.[17]

A part of the history of teacher strikes can be seen in Table 7.1. Most of those strikes occurred in September and February, the critical start-up times for schools.

Table 7.1

Summary of Teacher Strikes by State, July, 1960-June, 1974[18]

State	Number of Strikes	Estimated Number of Personnel Involved	Estimated Number of Man-Days Lost
Alaska	1	500	250
Arizona	1	801	4,005
California	37	43,891	407,376
Colorado	9	6,203	45,472
Connecticut	31	17,562	88,339
Delaware	4	1,709	5,268
District of Columbia	6	9,646	77,846
Hawaii	1	9,000	117,000
Florida	4	32,000	423,800
Georgia	3	179	913
Idaho	1	300	300
Illinois	101	95,488	619,126
Indiana	19	33,932	147,495
Iowa	2	209	592

(cont. on next page)

State	Number of Strikes	Estimated Number of Personnel Involved	Estimated Number of Man-Days Lost
Kentucky	7	55, 060	191, 810
Kansas	1	81	1, 944
Louisiana	4	2, 607	16, 271
Maryland	10	18, 465	199, 725
Massachusetts	13	10, 730	57, 450
Michigan	227	89, 688	695, 089
Minnesota	2	2, 096	30, 960
Missouri	14	9, 916	130, 221
Montana	3	948	2, 546
Nevada	2	3, 200	5, 600
New Hampshire	7	1, 992	17, 666
New Jersey	57	27, 916	330, 108
New Mexico	3	3, 058	15, 218
New York	61	143, 051	3, 341, 208
North Dakota	1	200	4, 400
Ohio	122	30, 434	92, 988
Oklahoma	5	24, 822	26, 932
Oregon	1	210	1, 890
Pennsylvania	171	100, 432	1, 140, 611
Rhode Island	23	10, 770	66, 696
South Carolina	1	850	850
South Dakota	1	441	3, 969
Tennessee	7	1, 095	8, 744
Texas	1	9, 000	18, 000
Utah	4	12, 325	24, 950
Washington	7	2, 267	9, 315
West Virginia	3	114	272
Wisconsin	39	9, 920	102, 295
Total	1, 017	823, 108	8, 475, 510

Many states have passed legislation prohibiting strikes by public employees. The statutes provide for discharge of, and loss of employment rights by, public employees participating in a strike. The New York Supreme Court has upheld the constitutionality of a "no strike" statute (in the Taylor Law), but there has been no ruling by the United States Supreme Court in this field. Moreover, the teacher strikes in the early 1960s in New York City revealed that punitive portions of state statutes might be set aside in mutually developed settlements, and that the membership rank and file might be relieved of the threats posed by state statute. Teacher strikes (which were initially called sanctions) in Florida in the latter 1960s led to exactly the opposite result as courts upheld boards which implemented the punitive portions of the state's anti-strike laws. The uncertainty about consequences despite statutory similarities emphasizes the key position occupied by the small group participating in negotiations and representing the entire employee group. The negotiating team must possess good small-group skills.

Persons involved in negotiations or addressing grievances might be identified as small-group members. Focusing upon the labor problem, there is likely to be a substantial difference among members, that difference being the basis for two groups blended together into one group for one endeavor, i. e., problem resolution. Acknowledging some disharmony, the labor-management negotiating group is, nonetheless, obligated to attempt to move toward problem resolution. Adversarial roles cannot be allowed to overshadow the necessity to follow some valid decision-making method. The problem must be precisely articulated; ambiguity must be overcome; information must be gathered and analyzed; discussants must be amenable to listen, compromise, and carry out other techniques which have proven successful as groups have moved toward consensus. Many of the small-group techniques generally thought of as suitable for groups centering upon harmony may also be advantageously used by groups which are adversarial in nature.

Communication is one key. Messages must be kept clean and uncluttered. To some degree, it is true that strikes occur after communications at a verbal level fail, for then workers may feel that some more intense communications system may "turn the trick."

The strike as a labor relations "weapon" has been fashioned out of the motivation that action should be focused upon things which are likely to have a high money yield for the participants. There is a widespread, if implicit, creed in American society which states that the common good will be extended if wages and salaries are maximized and increased at every contract renewal. At the same time, society gives lip service--but only lip service--to other characteristics which society holds in esteem, such as moral or aesthetic characteristics. Such a narrow viewpoint is encouragement to employers and employees, alike, to adopt the short view over the long view as plans for both the union and the employing organization are developed. A social action may be degrading or immoral, but if some social segment sees it as carrying potential for economic gain, it will very likely exist, unless it is unlawful. If, upon trial, it seems effective, it will not only exist, it will prosper. In a theoretical sense, then, the strike as the work-stoppage weapon can be seen as a device conceived very narrowly, which excludes moral and aesthetic considerations, but which has stood the test of improving someone's economic lot. [19]

This is the generally held perception of the reason for the strike. It may be that teachers as an occupational category are an exception; the research cited earlier, at least, seems to indicate that. Some other occupations may be exceptions to the general rule, as well; certainly, public employment envelopes a wide spectrum of occupational types. But for all of the individuality and the possible exceptions, the strike is generally seen as a weapon of economic advancement.

Because courts have stated that a doctrine under which public employees may strike is, in effect, a real transfer of power statutorily vested in public officials, courts will enjoin strikes. Injunctions have been issued against unions and officers stipulating that they may not order, participate in, or encourage strikes against governmental units. The point is that governmental services are essential and it is not the prerogative of private citizens, who are coincidentally members of some union, to usurp power and disrupt essential services.

Courts have made it clear that governmental boards, because they are bound by statutory limits, may not exceed those limits and agree to strikers' demands, even in instances where the board may be in sympathy with the demands. That is, such agreements are susceptible of suit, and if challenged in a court may be set aside. Additionally, courts have claimed that "... there is an adequate opportunity for employees to achieve their aims by methods short of the strike--through legislation and resorting to grievance machinery. "[20]

Two court cases from the same state offer unusual views on strikes by public employees. In Manchester v. the Manchester Teachers' Guild (1957) the New Hampshire Supreme Court stated:

There is no doubt that the legislature is free to provide by statute that public employees may enforce their right to collective bargaining by arbitration or strike.

In the Timberlane Regional School District v. Timberlane Regional Education Association (1974), the same court refused to issue an injunction against striking teachers who picketed the school and ultimately forced the closing of the junior and senior high schools. The court noted that denial of the right to strike ". . . has the effect of heavily weighing the collective bargaining process in favor of government." The New Hampshire legislature had failed to develop adequate methods for resolution of impasse, and in the absence of such helpful legislation the court put the onus upon the lawmakers for "forcing" teachers into an illegal strike as one bargaining technique beyond impasse. One or two other state courts have held similarly, but much more frequently, courts have a record of issuing injunctions against striking public employees.

An example of rather extreme court action against public employees can be seen in the matter of the Newark Teachers Union Local 481... (1972) heard by the Superior Court of New Jersey. There, the court did issue an injunction, ordering the union to return to work. The order was violated. The union was charged with contempt of court. The court pointed out that citizens may not defy court orders and take the law into their own hands. A fine which accumulated to $270,000 was levied against the local union, and fines and jail sentences were meted against officers and members identified as leaders in the contempt action. Finally, the court offered a little advice to the state's legislature, suggesting that if public employee strikes were to be prohibited by law, then some sort of binding procedures for compulsory settlement of deadlocked dispute seemed in order. Binding arbitration has not been found to be an unlawful delegation of power away from public governing boards, and may be the procedure which is needed.

Strike Bans

Although it is generally illegal for public employees to strike, the strike often appears to be an attractive negotiations "weapon." For that reason, public employees need a clear understanding of the technique. The penalties for illegal striking can be very severe.

In the absence of a right to strike, what techniques should be made available to assist parties who are at stalemate? At least three alternatives are now used somewhere in the nation, legally:

1. limited use of the strike,
2. compulsory arbitration,
3. legislative intervention.

A strike ban necessitates consideration of what to do if workers strike anyway, illegally. What penalties should be imposed? Should the penalties be assessed against the whole union, the union leader, or someone else?[21]

Conceivably, it may sometimes be a good tactic for the employee's negotiating team just to talk about the possibility of a strike. The goal would be to stimulate the governing board to start talking among themselves, to bring about faster action by the board. But there are other possible consequences, too. If talking strike does no good, then the bluff has failed and the next action would have to be to strike, or fold. The strike has been used effectively in the private sector; it is tempting to hold the same expectation for the public sector. Strikes have been used in the public sector, but with obviously great variations in effectiveness. Although there once was a time when striking by public employees was considered unethical, that time has apparently passed. Its effects are so uncertain and far reaching, however, that consideration of its use to obtain concessions must be measured carefully against legal, economic, political, and professional effects. It is surely the most indelicate and least sophisticated technique for dispute settlement which can seriously be advocated as a viable late-twentieth-century labor-management relations technique. To ban strikes by public employees, while providing statutorily for other resolution techniques, speaks to the desirability of uninterrupted public services.

References

1. Pierce, Lawrence. "Teachers, Organizations and Bargaining," in Public Testimony on Public Schools, by the National Committee for Citizens in Education. Berkeley: McCutcheon Publishing, 1975, pp. 137-138.

2. Weitzman, Joan. The Scope of Bargaining in Public

Employment. New York: Praeger Publishers, 1975, pp. 49-50.

3.   "Is the Strike Obsolete as a Union Weapon?" U.S. News and World Report, June 25, 1973, p. 70.

4.   Hazard, William R. Education and the Law. New York: Free Press, 1971, p. 289.

5.   Elam, Stanley. "Strikes or Sanctions," Education Digest, January 1963, p. 2.

6.   Moskow, Michael H. Teachers and Unions. Philadelphia: University of Pennsylvania Industrial Research Unit, 1966, p. 103.

7.   Pierce, op. cit., p. 140.

8.   Ross, Arthur M. "The Natural History of the Strike," in Industrial Conflict, ed. by Arthur Kornhauser and others. New York: McGraw-Hill, 1954, p. 23.

9.   Ibid., p. 24.

10.   Commens, John R. History of Labor in the United States. New York: Macmillan, 1918, p. 125.

11.   Brecher, Jeremy. Strike. San Francisco: Straight Arrow Books, 1972, p. 1.

12.   Twenty-Fifth Annual Report of the Commissioner of Labor, 1910: Industrual Education. Washington, D.C.: Government Printing Office, 1911, pp. 377-378.

13.   Zeigler, Harmon. "Teacher Militancy: An Analysis of the Strike-Prone Teacher," in Emerging Issues in Education, ed. by James E. Bruno. Lexington, Mass.: D. C. Heath, 1972, pp. 118-119.

14.   Ibid., pp. 106-107.

15.   Mayer, Allan L. "Who's in Charge? Public Employee Unions Press for Policy Role; State and Cities Balk," Wall Street Journal, September 7, 1972, p. 1.

16.   National Education Association. NEA Reporter, October, 1977.

17. New York Times, October 2, 1977, p. 40.

18. Rynecki, Steven B. "Can Compulsory Arbitration Work in Education ... ?" Journal of Law and Education, October, 1974, pp. 648-649.

19. Schumacher, E. F. Small Is Beautiful. New York: Harper and Row, 1973, pp. 43-48.

20. Moskow, op. cit., p. 53.

21. Kheel, Theodore W. "Introduction: Background and History," in Public Employee Unions, ed. by A. Lawrence Chickering. Lexington, Mass.: D. C. Heath, 1976, p. 10.

Chapter 8

EQUAL EMPLOYMENT OPPORTUNITIES

Introduction

From a time of job scarcity, of esteem for the family, of expectation of self-sufficiency, and of independence from governmental support (welfare), there developed the concept that males should have preference over females in job selection. Also, that males should be paid more than females for performing the same job, because it took more money to maintain a family. If a society is to sustain and extend itself, obviously it must allow and encourage procreative unions. The family, within a legally contracted marriage, has been that designated union in this nation. A head of family could be identified, and to him "extra" pay for the larger expenses of wife and offspring was an entitlement. (This money flow might have been thought of as compensation to the female for her socially beneficial role as mother and homemaker. But, it was not, and it has not been so considered.) The cultural and social lineage of the family in this nation indicated the "naturalness" of this arrangement as it extended through the Great Depression in America. It was an arrangement in which two important generalizations prevailed. Now, they are less evident, or have been reversed.

1. Relative to today, stability within the marriage contract was high, and the divorce rate was low.

2. Relative to today, females worked within the household, and did not seek outside employment.

It seems appropriate to approach equality in public employment through some of the varied viewpoints and varied experiences of Americans.

In 1954, the Supreme Court addressed racial discrimination and emphasized equality as the chief criterion by which social adequacy could be judged, thus creating a new social atmosphere in the nation. The Court called for all deliberate speed in the radical revision of institutions, and implied an obligation for restitution. The speed or slowness with which major social and economic changes are accomplished are judged very differently by political conservatives and political radicals. Both categories of citizens, however, must be part of the change, and of the rate of change. When citizens' expectations for immediate and radical change are raised, hope begins to dominate reality in the minds of the people for whom the change promises greatest advantage. Contrarily, fear may become dominant in the minds of others.

Equality is slippery, and has always been hard to grasp. A true definition of equality, in a social setting, is uncertain or variable; and, considered in a broad sense, it may be impossible for citizens to agree upon what it is. To understand equality in America, a reasonable starting point is Jefferson's pen: "... all [people] are created equal."

Central to democratic government in the United States is the principle that power can be held and governance exercised only with the consent of the governed. It has been a prevailing principle, an implicit declaration that all citizens should have an equal voice in governance.

But the idea of citizenship which embodies this conception has in the past 100 years been expanded to include equality not only in the public sphere, but in all other dimensions of social life as well-- equality before the law, equality of civil rights, equality of opportunity, even equality of results-- so that a person is able to participate fully, as a citizen, in the society. [1]

The concept of total equality for all citizens immediately raises a whole host of new questions for the society entertaining the concept. A few of those questions will be discussed briefly as a prelude to analyzing some applications of equal opportunities. Many of those applications have legal bases, and are integral parts of the collective bargaining process for public employees.

The principle of compensation for injustices committed in times past is a concept which is fraught with problems.

Finding it unworkable at an individual level, societies have accepted statutes of limitations, saying, in effect, that if a person has committed a wrong, he cannot be held accountable for that commission beyond a specified period of time. The principle of compensation is rendered further unworkable at the individual level by at least two other social principles: 1) offspring may not be held accountable for injustices committed by their parents and ancestors; 2) persons may not be held accountable for acts engaged in at some point in which, later on and after disengagement, are ruled to be unlawful.

Compensation, as advocated in contemporary American society, is not espoused at the individual level, but rather at a group level. That is, some social groups become labeled as perpetrators. This principle is not clearly manageable in its time constraints, but its economic implications are clear. For example, American blacks may charge American whites with the brutal crime of human slavery, and establish an expectation of compensation upon that charge, which is historically verifiable, but which could not involve any of the actual persons who were parties to the event. Or, likewise, native Americans could charge whites and others with fraud, misrepresentation, persecution, and a host of other crimes by which Indian territories were reduced, and those of other Americans enlarged.

In the current American political mileau, this principle of compensation is seldom articulated frankly, but if it were it would say, "You took something from me--or mine--too cheaply. Now, it is time for restitution." Politically, it is an attractive position, for it allows elected officials to approach many social problems via the theme of helping the downtrodden. The political application of the principle of compensation stipulated that the disadvantaged of society should be helped by those who are more fortunate, a concept deeply ingrained within the American culture. It is a concept which antedates, even, the altruistic story of the Good Samaritan, but with one major change: groups, not individuals, are the recipients of the compensatory acts.

The principle of compensation has found legal expression in concert with the evolving notion of total equality. Its legal bases can be found in rather recent legislation devoted to civil rights, equal educational and employment opportunities, restrictions calling for equal pay, and obligations for affirmative action to assure the accomplishment of total equality insofar as laws can guide citizens to its accomplishment.

Despite its current political popularity, the principle of compensation has several flaws which are becoming more apparent as time passes. Cool, rational questions are being asked which will, shortly, bear upon it in some way or another.

1. What groups should be compensated?

2. Who should be the members of those groups?

3. Who should be obligated to provide the compensation?

4. How far back in time should the applications of compensation be carried?

5. How can the contradictions between equality and compensation be reconciled?

These questions are only a sample from a longer list which may be raised from time to time. Equality of opportunity is not a stable, fixed condition. But, for now, in the latter 1970s, the American polity is committed to equality in a variety of discernible ways, and those affect conditions of employment.

Equality is elusive, both economically and culturally. Americans are free to compete; achievement is the pay-off, and acquisition and consumption is by degree, according to earnings. Culturally, Americans are free to express themselves, to choose without hindrance those styles and follow those inclinations which they most favor--and which they can afford. In that slightly mad mixup which exists in the minds of most, and in which wants tend to become needs, it is a politically viable position to talk about equality, guaranteed minima as indicators of equality, and restraints upon exploitation to assure equality. American society is characterized by many factors pressuring in the direction of citizen equality; but variations in ability, drive, and ambition among persons as they may be observed all over the world, and certainly in this nation, dictate that literal, total equality is highly improbable in any society resting upon a technological base. The demands of such a society translate into premiums for talent, without regard to whether the government is democratic or totalitarian.

Individuals and groups, seeing other citizens "ahead"

of them, define equality relatively. In that format it becomes a political credo in flux, a goal to be pursued through the political machinery of the society. That format is epitomized by the voter who, facing the political candidate, asks, "Yes, I know, but what have you done for me today?" There is no lack of claimants to preferential treatment from political bodies, and all may seek the label of equality. In the United States, the traditional governmental position has been that all citizens should be treated equally under the law. (An exception to that posture, preferential pay to heads of households, was cited earlier.) Currently, there is a new, strong effort to make people equal by treating them differentially before the law. Many rationales, many principles can be marshaled to support this position of preference for some, but it is a change of such great magnitude that its application has caused both eager anticipation and bitter resentment, as citizens view this change from their particular vantage point. The whole impinges upon and influences collective bargaining in the public sector.

Equality and Governmental Activity

It is appropriate to cite the Brown case (1954) as the primary landmark of vigorous activity by the federal government in the quest for citizen equality. There were many judicial antecedents, including Sweat (1946), McLaurin (1948), Sipuel (1946), and Gaines (1938). The legislative branch had not been entirely inactive in this regard, for post-bellum congresses had enacted civil rights acts in the 1860s and 1870s. Nonetheless, for understanding of the current participation of the federal government in the drive for equality, especially by minority groups, the Brown case is the logical starting point.

An indication of the interest of the legislative branch can be seen in some of the most directly influential statutes which have been enacted:

1. The Civil Rights Acts in 1957 and 1960 bore upon voting rights and school desegregation.

2. The Equal Pay Act of 1963 was devoted to eliminating pay differentials based upon tax.

3. The Civil Rights Act of 1964 was a comprehensive approach to problems of citizen equality.

4. The Civil Rights Act of 1968 forbade interstate travel with intent to incite riots; extended
constitutional rights to Indians (native Americans);
forbade discrimination in both the renting and sell-
ing of housing.

5. Other statutes in the latter 1960s included the
Voting Rights Act, the Model Cities Act, the Open
Housing Act, the creation of the Department of
Housing and Urban Development.

In short, the legislative reaction complemented the need for
action which had been indicated by the federal judiciary.
Some of the statutes deserve extensive treatment, for they
have sharply influenced the public employment setting.

The Civil Rights Act of 1964 (PL 88-252, July 2, 1964)

This comprehensive statute of several sections (titles)
extended the protection of voting rights, and provided for
equal employment opportunity without regard to race, color,
religion, sex, or national origin. It also called for desegregation of schools and public facilities, for equal access to
public accommodations, and for non-discrimination in feder-
ally assisted social programs. Title VII described unlawful
employment practices and established the Equal Employment
Opportunities Commission. (The Act did not affect employees
of state and local government agencies, including school districts, until 1972.) It provided for the enforcement of certain constitutional rights and provided relief in the preven-
tion of discrimination. [2]

As initially enacted, and with its subsequent amendments, this law has caused major changes in all employment
settings. Parts of this statute, excerpted here, show why
that is true.

SEC. 703. (a) It shall be an unlawful employment practice for an employer--
(1) to fail or refuse to hire or to discharge
any individual, or otherwise to discriminate
against any individual with respect to his
compensation, terms, conditions, or privi-
leges of employment, because of such individual's race, color, religion, sex, or national origin; or

(2) to limit, segregate, or classify his employees in any way which would deprive or tend to deprive any individual of employment opportunities or otherwise adversely affect his status as an employee, because of such individual's race, color, religion, sex, or national origin.

(b) It shall be an unlawful employment practice for an employment agency to fail or refuse to refer for employment, or otherwise to discriminate against, any individual because of his race, color, religion, sex, or national origin, or to classify or refer for employment any individual on the basis of his race, color, religion, sex, or national origin.

Comparable obligations and opportunities were made specific to labor organizations, i. e., the unions.

Title VII also called for the establishment of the Equal Employment Opportunities Commission. The five-member EEOC reports to the President and the Congress and was charged, generally, to investigate allegations of unlawful employment practices. Among its specific charges, the EEOC has the power

to furnish to persons subject to this title such technical assistance as they may request to further their compliance with this title or an order issued thereunder;

upon the request of (i) any employer, whose employees or some of them, or (ii) any labor organization, whose members or some of them, refuse or threaten to refuse to cooperate in effectuating the provisions of this title, to assist in such effectuation by conciliation or such other remedial action as is provided by this title;

to make such technical studies as are appropriate to effectuate the purposes and policies of this title and to make the results of such studies available to the public.

The Equal Employment Opportunities Act of 1972
(PL 92-261, March 24, 1972)

Growing out of the experiences of the EEOC, this Act

had as its goal the promotion of further equal opportunities in employment for American workers. The Act included all of the above Title VII and extended it with statements on enforcement, court action for non-compliance, and penalties-- including liability for back pay to plaintiffs who were success- ful in discrimination suits. It granted extensive investigatory power to the EEOC, and established the inter-cabinet EEOC Coordinating Council. [3] Its extensive length is an indicator of the comprehensiveness and specificity with which it treated the problem of equality in opportunities for employ- ment.

When Title VII was enacted, the EEOC was given no enforcement powers, to speak of. It could receive charges and investigate them, and upon determining them to be true, could attempt a remedy through persuasion. It could do little else. Under this Act of 1972 the EEOC was given broad powers under which it could follow up on charges through civil actions in federal courts. With all actions for individual remedy on strict timelines, the Commission was also given, after two years, exclusive power to bring action for the elimination of unlawful discrimination practices in employment. That conferral of power took jurisdiction away from the Justice Department. The Act forbade discrimina- tion, but it did not require that affirmative action be taken to rectify existing imbalances. Explicitly, it stated that employment imbalance by race, sex, age, and so on is not a reason for preferential treatment of any group or indivi- dual, as a remedy. (Courts, however, have not construed that section literally, stating that it is not a "Ban on affir- mative relief against continuation of effects of past discrimi- nation. . . . ") With investigation, analysis, and enforcement in the same agency, and with its broad mandates over em- ployment, new record-keeping obligations necessarily have been imposed upon all employers. [4]

Parallel to the concerns evidenced by the legislative and judiciary branches are several of the Executive Orders which have been addressed to worker welfare. Some presi- dents have used them as political pressure devices, aimed to stimulate legislation. For example, by issuing E. O. 10988 (Executive Orders have been serially numbered since 1907), President Kennedy set a pattern with federal em- ployees which became a reference point for local government employees who wanted to organize and bargain--and in state after state they have persuaded legislators to pass the appro- priate statutes. Executive Orders have covered a wide range topically and some have revoked, modified, or consolidated the orders of previous presidents. Some are pertinent to equal employment in the public sector.

E. O. 10925. March 6, 1961. Establishing the President's Committee on Equal Employment Opportunities

After a brief review of conditions, needs, and intentions, the order called for non-discriminatory employment, and to advance that cause a committee was established, chaired by the Vice President. The committee was charged with surveillance, analysis, and reporting to the President. The objects of surveillance included federal, state and local government agencies, federal sub-contractors, and all affected labor unions. Investigation and enforcement powers were enumerated and a system of penalties and awards was described.

> ... Reports [to the President] shall be made at least once annually, and shall include specific references to the action taken and results achieved by each department and agency. The Chairman may appoint sub-committees to make special studies on a continuing basis. [5]

E. O. 10988. January 17, 1962. Employee-Management Cooperation in the Federal Service

With a rationale based upon personnel management research, and aimed at raising morale and production through participation, this order allowed for the organization of Federal Government employees. It was ordered that if employees exercised the right to organize, each federal agency should allow them to freely do so, without any penalties or reprisals.

> The head of each executive department and agency ... shall take such action, consistent with law, as may be required in order to assure that employees ... are apprised of the rights described ... and that no interference, restraining, coercion or discrimination is practiced ... to encourage or discourage membership in any employee organization.... An agency shall accord an employee organization formal recognition as the representative of its members. [6]

Proscribed were organizations which advocated the right to strike, or which discriminated against membership on the basis of race, color, creed, or national origin. Further, the employee's organization was excluded from some areas of the agency: mission, budget, organizational plan, personnel assignment, and the technology with which it did its work.

E. O. 11264. September 24, 1965.
Reassignment of Civil Rights Functions

This order was aimed at the elimination of job discrimination in federal agencies, and their sub-contractors. Resting on the Civil Rights Act of 1964, the order set forth general obligations, identified the enforcement responsibilities of various governmental departments, and explained the systems of penalties and awards. It also stipulated that

The head of each executive department and agency shall establish and maintain a positive program of equal employment opportunity for all civilian employees and applicants for employment within his jurisdiction.... The affirmative action process must not operate to restrict consideration to minorities and women only. [7]

E. O. 11375. October 13, 1967.
Equal Opportunity for Women in Federal Employment and Employment by Federal Contractors

This order directed attention to Title VII of the Civil Rights Act and to pertinent executive orders of previous years. It made explicit the desire that equal employment opportunity programs should allow for no discrimination on account of sex. Previous E. O. 11246 (1965) was amended as follows:

It is the policy of the Government of the United States to provide equal opportunity in federal employment for all qualified persons, to prohibit discrimination because of race, color, religion, sex, or national origin, and to promote the full realization of equal employment opportunity through a positive continuing program.... [8]

Affirmative Action Programs

Affirmative action is an extension and expansion of the concept of equal opportunity. From California, S. B. 179 (1977) demonstrates those expansion and extension factors well.

> ... discrimination in employment on the basis of race, sex, color, religion, age, physical handicap, ancestry or national origin [must be eliminated] in every aspect of personnel policy and practice employment, development, advancement and treatment of persons employed in the public school system, and [public schools] must promote the total realization of equal employment opportunity through a continuing affirmative action employment program.

The California approach is a good example of the kind of legislation passed by several states in response to the obligations for affirmative action which have been indicated by the federal government.

In 1976, the Equal Employment Opportunity Coordinating Council issued its policy statement, "Affirmative Action Programs for State and Local Government Agencies." That policy statement has been adopted widely, as local government agency boards have made it part of their own policies, usually adopting it in total. Asserting that evidence exists that equal access is the law but not always the practice, that policy statement called for remediation. The statement suggested "affirmative voluntary efforts on the part of public employers to assure that positions ... are genuinely and equally accessible to qualified persons, without regard to their sex, racial or ethnic characteristics." Specifically, programmatic steps through which exclusionary and discriminating effects could be addressed included the following:

> The establishment of a long-term goal, and short-range, interim goals and timetables for the specific job classifications, all of which should take into account the availability of basically qualified persons in the relevant job market;

> A recruitment program designed to attract qualified members of the group in question;

> A systematic effort to organize work and re-design

jobs in ways that provide opportunities for persons
lacking "journeyman"-level knowledge or skills to
enter and, with appropriate training, to progress
in a career field;

Revamping selection instruments or procedures
which have not yet been validated in order to reduce or eliminate exclusionary effects on particular
groups in particular job classifications;

The initiation of measures designed to assure that
members of the affected group who are qualified to
perform the job are included within the pool of
persons from which the selecting official makes
the selection;

A systematic effort to provide career advancement
training, both classroom and on-the-job, to employees locked into dead end jobs; and

The establishment of a system for regularly moni-
toring the effectiveness of the particular affirmative action program, and procedures for making
timely adjustments in this program where effectiveness is not demonstrated.

Finally, the Council suggested that no affirmative action plans
should require the selection of unneeded or unqualified persons, nor should persons be selected on the basis of sex,
color, race, religion or national origin. [9]

How is it determined that there is an employment inequality which might be addressed through affirmative action?
This is done at two levels, the general and the specific.
Data speaking to some aspects of the general condition of
inequality can be seen in Figure 8.1 and Table 8.1 (see both
on following page). Figure 8.1 indicates that despite stren-
uous efforts on the part of the federal government to assure
equality of opportunity, the disparity in unemployment rates
between whites and non-whites has continued at a remarkably
constant level over two decades. Table 8.1 indicates that
when attention is focused upon the Spanish-origin population,
their unemployment rates are at least as high as for non-
whites, and in 1975, were almost three times the rate for
whites. An inference which can be drawn from such general
data is that minority groups are still discriminated against
in employment. Many other inferences could be drawn, and

Figure 8. 1

UNEMPLOYMENT RATES OF WHITES AND NON-WHITES[10]
(annual averages)

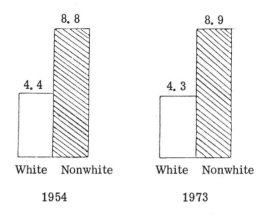

Table 8. 1

UNEMPLOYMENT RATES FOR SPANISH-ORIGIN POPULATION
UNITED STATES, 1960-1975[11]
(annual averages for ages 16 and older)

YEAR	MALE	FEMALE
1960	8. 3	10. 0
1969	5. 1	7. 5
1970	6. 2	8. 6
1971	8. 6	9. 2
1972	7. 4	10. 1
1973	6. 7	7. 7
1974	7. 2	9. 8
1975	13. 1	12. 2

there is no point in trying here to assess their relative accuracy. The point is that the inference of continued discrimination in employment has provided a rationale for affirmative action programs.

For the employer setting out to deal with affirmative

action requirements the first step is to examine the employment condition of the particular agency. Comparing that information with data from the manpower market, it becomes possible to discover the employer's precise position with regard to race, sex or some other factor. From such a data base, employers can move to establish the short-term, interim, and long-range goals which constitute the beginning of affirmative action programs. An example of such a specific data base is shown in Table 8. 2, in which every employee is assigned into a major occupational activity by sex, by race.

Surrounding affirmative action there is an aura of preferential treatment. That is difficult to resolve within the customary definition of equal. The Commission on Civil Rights said, in 1973, that affirmative action should include:

> Steps taken to remedy the grossly disparate staffing and recruitment patterns that are the present consequence of past discrimination and to prevent the occurrence of employment discrimination in the future. [13]

In Cramer v. Virginia Commonwealth University (1976) a federal district court ruled that the Civil Rights Act of 1964 absolutely forbade "... the use of sex quotas or goals in employment even to overcome an existing imbalance. " In the decision, the judge spoke about the use of "... unconstitutional means to achieve an unconstitutional end, " and overturned one governmental agency's affirmative action plan after it had been approved by federal officials.

Obviously, there is some discord over the application of affirmative action programs. Part of that derives from the use of data which have been separated from specific cases and generalized. Much of that discord arises from other circumstances. In bargaining, the employer must not bargain away those management rights which must be preserved to keep the employer in compliance with affirmative action obligations. In public schools, for example, that consideration would have a practical effect upon promotions and any kind of money advancement, and on how those matters could be handled.

Equal Employment in Contracts

People find jobs in a variety of ways, and those ways

Table 8.2

University of Nebraska at Omaha[12]

Equal Opportunity Compliance Survey Summary for UNO

M.O.A.	Male					Female				
	White	Black	Spanish	Indian	Oriental	White	Black	Spanish	Indian	Oriental
Admin./Managerial	43	2	0	0	0	5	2	0	0	0
Instructional	329	6	4	0	1	89	7	2	0	0
Professional	67	2	2	0	0	29	6	0	0	0
Unclassified	0	0	0	0	0	0	0	0	0	0
Technical	16	1	0	0	0	3	0	0	0	0
Clerical/Secretary	16	2	0	0	1	173	15	1	0	0
Crafts/Trades	20	0	0	0	0	13	4	0	0	0
Service Workers	81	4	0	1	0	12	9	0	0	1

Total .... 983 (Non-Citizens 14)

change from time to time. For example, in public employment there was a time when the "spoils system" prevailed. The winner of an election would fire all who had not supported his or her candidacy, and hire people who had. Characteristically resulting in low morale and high anxiety, the "spoils system" was eventually replaced by civil service. Civil service was designed to discover ability among applicants and to provide for continuity in their performance as employees after having been hired. Many of the basic tenets of the current understanding of equal employment opportunity were embodied in civil service.

Present-day employees of such major political units as states, cities, and school districts find their assurances of equal treatment as a part of the contract which is negotiated for them by their union. Most--but not all--such contracts contain clauses which translate the legal responsibilities into specifics for the local job setting. These excerpts from three different contracts stand as good examples of contract clauses which speak to equal opportunities.

The contract between the Detroit Board of Education and the Detroit Federation of Teachers, for July 1, 1975-June 30, 1977, contained the following clause:

II. FAIR PRACTICES

A. In accord with Board policy, no person or persons, departments or divisions responsible to the Board shall discriminate against any employee on the basis of race, creed, color, national origin, sex, marital status, or membership in, or association with the activities of, the Union.
B. In accord with its Constitution, the Union will admit persons to membership without discrimination on the basis of race, creed, color, national origin, sex or marital status.
C. The Union and the Board agree to continue to work affirmatively in implementing their mutual objective of effective integration of faculties and student bodies in all Detroit schools.

The New York agreement covered 60,000 teachers and was negotiated between the Board of Education and the UFT #2, American Federation of Teachers, AFL-CIO. Covering the three years, September 9, 1972 to September 9, 1975, it included the following fair practices clause:

ARTICLE II
Fair Practices

The Union agrees to maintain its eligibility to represent all teachers by continuing to admit persons to membership without discrimination on the basis of race, creed, color, national origin, sex or marital status and to represent equally all employees without regard to membership or participation in, or association with the activities of, any employee organization.

The Board agrees to continue its policy of not discriminating against any employee on the basis of race, creed, color, national origin, sex, marital status or membership or participation in, or association with the activities of, any employee organization.

The Board agrees that it will not require any teacher to complete an oath or affirmation of loyalty unless such requirement is established by law.

A slight variation can be seen in the contract negotiated for blue-collar nonsupervisory workers in Hawaii. The contract was between the American Federation of State, County and Municipal Employees, and several political agencies in the state, effective July 1, 1974 to June 30, 1976. Two separate parts of the contract spoke to the topic of discrimination:

Section 3. DISCRIMINATION.

3. 01 The Employer and the union agree that neither party will discriminate against any employee because of membership or non-membership or lawful activity in the Union or on the basis of race, color, creed, sex, or lawful political activity.

. . .

Section 1. RECOGNITION.

1. 03 The Employer and the Union agree that they will not interfere with the right of any employee to join or refrain from joining the Union. The Employer will make known to all new employees that they will secure no advantage or more favorable consideration or any form of privilege because of membership or non-membership in the Union.

A major issue in differentiated treatment of employees has centered upon wages or salary paid. Teachers represent the largest single occupational category among public employees. Many years ago, teachers in public elementary and secondary school were successful in eliminating pay differentials based upon sex. The single salary schedule has many strong points. One of these is that the schedule for payment of salary is governed by function, and not by personality; that is, there is not one salary schedule for one person or one group of employees, and still another for some other group. The schedule indicates the level of compensation for a given function with but two variables--preparation and experience, and those are attainable at levels of equality by all employees. Not all public employee groups have salary delivery systems which are insensitive to sex, race, age, religion, and national origin. Well established as a national practice, the long-popular single salary schedule anticipated much of the Civil Rights Act of 1964, and is a "natural" part of the public school employer's compliance posture--a "natural" part of every teacher contract.

Cases

After contracts have been concluded and employees are at work, disputes have arisen in which discrimination has been alleged. In the following seven cases from various states, employees have charged discrimination by age, sex, or race. They stand as good examples of the need for care in contract administration. All except one are cases which were resolved at arbitration.

Barnes v. Schlesinger (and Hoffman) (VA, 1976)

In a case which alleged discrimination by race, Barnes and Williams, plaintiffs, showed that thirty-four whites and no blacks had been promoted between July 31, 1972 and July 31, 1974. The court noted that "While this pattern appears prima facie discriminatory, it is tempered by the correlative fact that there were no more than five blacks employed ... out of a total workforce of approximately 200 during that period." The court denied relief to the plaintiffs but provided injunctive relief regarding the recruitment of blacks. This special facility of the U. S. Army was ordered to increase its black work force by two per cent per year until ten per cent of the workforce was black, or the percentage employed equalled the percentage of blacks in the surrounding communities. The recruitment obligations were made specific, and the employer was directed to keep records of all applicants for employment--those hired and those not hired--by name and race. In every case, reasons for hiring or refusing to hire were to be on file. In effect, the court accepted the charge of discrimination in hiring. The goal of ten per cent black in four years was imposed by the court.[14]

Seattle Community College and SCC Federated Teachers (WA, 1971)

With the assistance of the AAA, an arbiter was selected to hear the grievance which, in part, hinged upon this question: Was the grievant, a long-term employee and candidate for the post of department chairman, discriminated against by the president when a younger person was selected to the post? The arbitrator heard evidence of procedures for selection in which the choice was finally reduced to the grievant and the person selected. The factors in selection included academic preparation, suitable management experience, and outside recommendations. Actual selection was the responsibility of the institution's president, and the arbiter could find no evidence of bias against age.[15]

Niagara County Community College and Faculty Association of NCCC (NY, 1976)

The teacher in this case had received four successive one-year contracts. A fifth was not offered. The college contended that nothing was arbitrable; i.e., term contracts expire and some are not renewed. The arbitrator ruled that the college lacked a contractually based code governing student-teacher relationships, but that it was due to her activity in that area that the teacher's contract was not renewed. Therefore, she had been discharged, and the incident became arbitrable. The teacher had undergone a major change in personality, having become an aggressive exponent of a kind of militant feminism after her initial hiring. Evidence indicated prejudice against her by her male colleagues. The contract stipulated that the work agreement would be applied "without regard to race, creed, religion, color, national origin, sex, age, nepotism or marital status." Although this was a term contract, its non-renewal was tainted with discrimination by sex. Employees may not be discharged

for their opinions which are eccentric or strange. Unortho-
dox beliefs are not grounds for discharge, unless the employer can prove that they detract from the necessary minimum quality level of performing as an instructor. [16]

Byron Area Schools and Michigan Education Association (MI, 1976)

In order to hire a part-time male counselor, it was
necessary to reduce the time spent in counseling by a female
employee. She was reassigned to teach English half-time.
Pay was not a concern in this grievance. She had been a
full-time counselor for four years and the total counseling
load in this school was one person, full-time. The arbitrator heard testimony which supported the need for counseling by both sexes in a coed high school and claimed that
both boys and girls were hesitant to discuss frankly and
openly all their problems with counselors of the opposite sex.
There was no reduction in pay and the teaching assignment
was in English, a subject which the grievant had taught and
for which she held a certificate. The arbitrator ruled that,
in certain jobs, it was permissible to prefer a male, if the
employer could prove that such would enhance the whole instructional endeavor. No bias or discrimination against the
grievant was found. [17]

Massachusetts Port Authority and Teamster's Local #157 (MS, 1977)

The grievant was the first female hired to the position in question. Over five months, eighty-four performance
reports had been filed, at least thirty-eight of which were
derogatory in some degree. As a regular part-time employee, the grievant was accorded all necessary procedural
safeguards. The employee was terminated, charged with
insubordination. Specifically, the employee consistently
punched the register late, so that supervisors could not tell
if her receipts actually exceeded what the register tallied.
Late punching made it possible for toll takers to be "on the
take," and this was a grievous operational defect in the employer's view. The charge stipulated that, despite warnings,
she continued to perform "well below minimum standards of
efficiency and responsiveness to orders." The arbiter ruled
that she was not unjustly terminated, and there was no discrimination on the basis of sex. [18]

Stockton Unified Schools and Stockton
Teachers Association (CA, 1976)

This contract contained a comprehensive non-discrimination clause. The grievant was a female employee who had achieved tenure as a teacher, who was later designated as a counselor, and who was finally reassigned as a classroom teacher, at no change in pay. The reassignment was grieved as discriminatory. The association argued that the reassignment worsened an already adverse male-female ratio among the counselors. The arbiter viewed teaching and counseling as equivalent positions, upon evidence and testimony, and rejected the ratio argument because if a male had been reassigned it would have worsened the sex ratio among the teachers. The arbiter acknowledged the possibility of conflict between the non-discrimination clause and an affirmative action program which called for preferential treatment, but stipulated its unapplicability in situations where promotion is not involved. Teaching and counseling were labeled as functionally equivalent; the grievant was not discriminated against. [19]

Fall River School Committee and FR
Educators Association (MS, 1976)

The grievant was a white female tenured teacher with six years in the schools, working under a contract which stated that "in filling vacancies, preference will be given, in the case of comparable qualifications, to teachers already employed...." In the district's drive to accomplish a racial balance obligation, the grievant was denied a transfer request to a position which instead was given to a teacher with a bachelor's degree and a few weeks of experience. There was some testimony of incapacity on the part of the experienced teacher, but its source was in a single comment from the principal to the department head, the latter having never visited the grievant's classroom. Personnel records held no indication of incapacity. She was denied return to her former position on the basis that it would be filled by a black male. The arbiter did not pronounce that discrimination on the basis of sex had occurred, but did order the school to place the grievant in a high school science teaching position at the first vacancy, "but no later than September, 1977."[20] (Conceivably, then, she was not in a teaching position during the 1976-77 school year.)

Uncertainties in Equality

The uncertainties which surround equality may be a commentary upon the American ability to assimilate major social changes, or it may be more a commentary upon human nature. Social discord has followed the actions of government--especially, the federal judiciary and legislative--in directing citizens toward prescribed equality of opportunities. Domestic violence and destruction have been recent developments to the nation in the twentieth century, in both cause and intensity. The tensions which develop in the implementation of equalizing opportunities in employment surface in many places. In the vigorous pursuit of equality of opportunity led by such agencies as the Office of Civil Rights, the Department of Health, Education and Welfare, and the Equal Employment Opportunities Commission, and especially through programs calling for affirmative action, some new terminology has come to the fore. Preference has been labeled affirmative action and, sometimes, reverse discrimination; or, as one social commentator named it, affirmative discrimination. [21] American society is confused and uncertain about the practical meanings of equality and discrimination. Two cases from the realm of higher education amply demonstrate the confusion and uncertainties, yet not in a hostile, but in a rational setting--before the United States Supreme Court. They are the DeFunis and Bakke cases, and they are relevant to a consideration of equality in employment for many reasons, not the least of which is that they have to do with admission to professional schools--a necessary prelude to employment in many occupational categories.

DeFunis v. Odegarrd (WA, 1974)

Marco DeFunis, a white male Jew, was denied a place in the entering class of the law school at the University of Washington. A magna cum laude baccalaureate holder, he showed that he ranked higher on the school's own entrance tests than did thirty-eight persons identified as belonging to a minority group, who were admitted under a special minorities admission plan. In early hearings, DeFunis won a court order for his admission. The university appealed, and the state's supreme court ruled against DeFunis, holding that the state could use racial classification "... in a compensatory way to promote integration." DeFunis was allowed to continue in school, and appealed to the Supreme Court. Several questions, some of which were rhetorical, were raised for the Court's consideration, including the following:

1. May a public school insist upon differentiated student assignments to promote integration?

2. May a public school official conclude that racially integrated schools are a good thing?

3. May preferential treatment be extended to members of designated minority groups?

4. Is there a difference in obligations for desegregated education between elementary-secondary schools and post-graduate professional schools?

5. Should Jews be a designated minority for preferential treatment?

DeFunis had been allowed to stay in law school, and by the time the Court was ready to pronounce, he was at point of graduation. Noting this, the Court chose to pronounce that the case was moot; i. e., purely academic with no practical meaning. The Court decided not to decide.

University of California, Davis v. Bakke (CA, 1978)

In a case similar to the DeFunis case, Allan Bakke was a white male who was denied admission to the university's medical college at Davis. Before the state's supreme court, he showed that he ranked higher on the admission tests than some of the minority students who were admitted, and that sixteen per cent of the positions were reserved for a special admissions program available only to persons of designated minority groups. The state ruled against the university after having measured its admissions program against the Fourteenth Amendment, and finding that its program accorded preference on the basis of race, an impermissible preference. The university has appealed to the U. S. Supreme Court. Several questions being considered by the Court include the following:

1. Does the equal protection clause apply literally to all individuals?

2. Can the equal protection clause be applied selectively, allowing for amelioration of the effects of past discrimination by race?

3. Within the concept of flexible admissions criteria, can race be one criterion?

4. When racial quotas are specified as a part of a special selection program, do those quotas, by themselves, invalidate any program which might be devised?

In a June 1978 decision, the Court pronounced on two questions: it ruled that Bakke had been unlawfully denied admission, and that university admissions programs could appropriately include race (minorities) as one factor in the selective admission of students. Each decision was split, 5-4; the nine justices wrote six different opinions. The precise bearing this case will have upon equal employment opportunities is not immediately apparent.

The equal opportunity/affirmative action statements which have been incorporated into hiring practices, and, by way of extended policy, into contracts, cannot remain stable over a long period of time. Those statements have been developed through the nation's experiences in the courts and the legislatures, and with the implementing regulations developed by the administering agencies. The statements must change. The direction of change is not, however, perfectly predictable. As a consequence of the tensions in society, it seems unlikely that the change will be consistent and in a single direction. In the meantime, each contract must reflect the prevailing law in regard to recruitment, hiring, transfer, promotion, and dismissal--the personnel management functions which must be bias-free, and which so strongly influence any attempts at equality of employment.

References

1. Bell, Daniel. The Cultural Contradictions of Capitalism. New York: Basic Books, Inc., 1976, p. 11.

2. United States Statutes at Large. Volume 78. Washington: Superintendent of Documents, 1965, pp. 241-268.

3. Ibid., Volume 86. Washington: Superintendent of Documents, 1972, pp. 235-381.

4. Bureau of National Affairs. The Equal Employment Opportunity Act of 1972. Washington: The Bureau, 1973, pp. 3-7.

5. Code of Federal Regulations, Title 3--The President (1959-1963). Washington: Superintendent of Documents, 1964, pp. 448-454.

6. Ibid., pp. 521-538.

7. Weekly Compilation of Presidential Documents. Washington: Superintendent of Documents, Volume 1, #9, September 27, 1965, pp. 305-307.

8. Ibid., Volume 3, #41, October 16, 1967, pp. 14-37.

9. Federal Register. Doc 76-26675, September 10, 1976.

10. Bureau of the Census. Social and Economic Status of the Black Population in the United States. Current Population Reports, series P-23 #48 (1974), table 28.

11. United States Commission of Civil Rights. Last Hired, First Fired--Layoffs and Civil Rights. Washington: The Commission, 1977, p. 80.

12. University of Nebraska. "Policy Statement and Affirmative Action Program." Lincoln, NE: The University, 1974, p. 11.

13. United States Commission on Civil Rights, op. cit., p. 14.

14. Government Employee Relations Reports. 694:6-7, February 7, 1977.

15. 30 - Arbitration in the Schools - 10

16. 81 - AIS - 17

17. 81 - AIS - 21

18. Labor Arbitration in Government - 1770

19. 76 - AIS - 6

20. 79 - AIS - 5

21. Glazer, Nathan. Affirmative Discrimination. New York: Basic Books, Inc., 1975.

Chapter 9

JOB SECURITY

The Need

In the small, person-to-person employment relations which were typical in the early nineteenth-century industrial settings, a common understanding was carried over from the artist-agrarian work relationships. It was one of mutual sovereignty. That is, the employee was not indentured, but was free to quit the job; likewise, the employer was free to discharge the employee. In Commonwealth v. Moore (1828), the prevailing arguments reflected the employer's freedom of action.

> ... [the employers] had an undisputed right to discharge any workman ... when they conceived his continuance was no longer conducive to their interest ... they were at perfect liberty to dismiss every journeyman [tailors] ... the discharge was a perfect right, without assignment or even existence of reason. Let him be without reason ... let it be caprice. Still it was a right, with which no man or set of men must be permitted to interfere....

This relationship, in which it was emphasized that the employer was free to dismiss the worker, was very typical of the nineteenth century. [1] That situation produced its own history and its own lingering reaction among all employees, including those who work for public agencies.

Surveys have consistently revealed that teachers see teaching, despite some occupational inadequacies, as a generally desirable job. Such a perception gives rise to strong employee feelings of urgency when job security is considered.

Some of those strong feelings may have their base in the oc-cupational inadequacies, too. Historically, teacher contracts were discriminatory, and frequently punitive as well.

In 1977, the average teacher salary was $13,297. From 1973-74 through 1975-76, the Consumer Price Index rose 24.3 per cent; in that same period, the average teacher salary rose 23.4 per cent. Speaking at the 1977 National Education Association Convention, the NEA executive secretary, Terry Herndon, observed that in the 1976-77 school year, "... Nearly one-third of secondary school teachers still deal with 150 or more students each day."

At that same convention, Jerry Wurf, the AFSCME president, remarked that

> ... public employees are having to deal with anti-public service politics in this country, and it is affecting the well being of every public worker and every American. Society is not as rich or as reasonable as it used to be, or as we thought.

The Coalition of American Public Employees (CAPE) was identified as a job enhancement-job security strength, just upon the basis of power in numbers. CAPE includes NEA, AFSCME, the National Association of Social Workers, and the National Treasury Employees Union.[2]

American society provides for the public interest and welfare through special mission public agencies. Operational funds for such public agencies are drawn from revenues collected through government's use of taxing powers. Characteristically, local public agencies get their funds from taxes which are levied and collected locally, and augmented from other money sources. (Reform of this traditional tax-ing pattern is very uneven among the states, but it is still the prevailing pattern.) Fiscal collapse of a local public agency is possible. When a tax levy is increased but col-lections fall, a net revenue is yielded which may be less than that collected on an identical levy in preceding years. The relationships between job security and agency financial sta-bility are obvious; financial exigency may be a reason for personnel reductions. When levies rise to the point that the tax base moves away to another, more economical location, the public agency is in trouble. So are its employees. Ne-gotiators need to be alert to this factor--its imminence or remoteness--in their locality.

A recent example of fiscal instability occurred in New York City. Services of a number of public agencies had been increasing; costs for those services had increased, too. In 1976 it became apparent that all revenues would be insufficient to pay all public agency operational costs. Personnel costs comprise the highest cost category in public agency budgets. The "natural" place to look for possibilities of cost reduction is in the highest cost category of the budget. The result in New York was that people were dismissed for reasons of financial exigency. For example, the City University of New York dismissed over 1, 000 faculty members, most of whom received no more than thirty days notice. Throughout the city, payrolls were trimmed and services reduced as public agencies cut costs, bringing costs into congruence with revenues. Unless public employees are willing to work as volunteers or with uncertain salary prospects, budget planning must give realistic attention to revenue development. Employees must carry out some of that planning, both for their own information and in conjunction with their effort to form the money demands which they will carry into negotiations.

Every worker seeks job security against every foreseeable adverse contingency. It is always high on the list of union goals. In some years, job security has been union goal number one, superseding wages, whenever workers felt threatened about job loss. Collectively, that is a reaction by workers who, as individual consumers, have done their part in building the massive private debt which U. S. citizens have accumulated, and who are aware of their need for a steady cash flow.

To purchase a house with a down-payment of ten per cent, or less, and the remainder of the price carried in a long-term mortgage, with interest, is a strong motivator toward job security. Monthly payments are dependent upon a monthly wage. This illustration of the debt carried for housing is real enough to have meaning for most adult Americans, but it is actually much too simple. Other debts and expenses come regularly, too. In the current American economic pattern, workers consume at comparatively high rates, and are encouraged to translate wants into needs--and then, buy.

The simpler expansionist period of the American westward movement has passed. In those earlier times, the collapse of an individual's economic world frequently meant relocation and a new start. Over several decades, citizens moved to another place where land was free to those who would live on it, use it, and develop it. That opportunity, through which food and shelter could be secured, could hardly be called job security, but it was an escape route toward a new opportunity, a new start; and economic security was the goal.

The complexity of society has increased. Underdeveloped, desirable land spaces have disappeared. The magnitude of the private debt has increased dramatically in the twentieth century, and especially since WW II. To "pay off" a debt demands a flow of cash without serious interruption. Every American worker, from the highest paid executives to the lowest paid menials, strives for some kind of job security. Or, if not security to a specific job, economic security in some form or another.

The drive for job security has called for the invention of new employment relationships--and new unemployment provisions. Many of those inventions have been enacted into laws. Many have been expressed as clauses in negotiated contracts. Some job protection devices have been pronounced by courts, particularly in cases where workers have been dismissed without statements of just cause.

There are some paradoxical twists in the drive toward job security. Not only do workers want job security, they want it at some particular compensation level. A major economic difference between the public and private sectors has operated to the detriment of public employees and the economy, generally. In private industry, where a product is the typical goal of the organization, UAW workers, for example, may demand and receive a ten per cent wage increase. Labor costs comprise about thirty per cent of the costs in the production of automobiles. The rise in unit costs from that ten per cent increase, then, is about three per cent. If productivity also rises three per cent, and that is frequently the case, then no inflationary increase had occurred.

Public agencies are labor-intensive; personnel costs commonly run about seventy-five per cent of the total costs. If firefighters, police, or teachers receive a ten per cent raise, that translates into a seven per cent or greater increase in costs. If productivity in the public agency also rises by three per cent, an optimistic expectation, then an inflationary gap of at least four per cent still remains. That

circumstance, coupled with the extended dimensions of services, has been a major cause in the increase, dispropor-
tionate within the national economic scene, of costs in state
and local government agencies. Thus agencies have been
propelled toward fiscal instability, emergency actions, and
service (i. e., personnel) reductions. The problem is one
of imbalance and has been seen at its worst with the 1976
and 1977 closings of public school systems that found themselves overcommitted and underfunded. [3]

This treatment of job security is brief. It has been
focused upon the economic necessity of a job as a money
source. Little attention has been given to unemployment
compensation, which has been a concern of unions in their
political endeavors. Hardly any attention has been devoted
to self-image and the effect upon it which comes from the
social stigma of unemployment. Although everyone may not
like to do what he or she does while at work, few would prefer to be hard-core non-workers drawing unemployment pay.
Job security, obviously, is a large topic unto itself; here,
the topic has been narrowed to a few of its conditions,
especially as they can be considered as economic aspects of
statutes and contracts.

Public workers, along with those in private industry,
want job security. Given their typical financial commitments,
it is surely fair to state that they need as much security in
their work as can reasonably be developed. To secure this
need, they must be aware of protections in the contract and
in state statutes, and of avenues of recourse in instances of
dispute. Likewise, management must be alert to new obligations, particularly procedural obligations, for contract
administration and personnel supervision.

Probation and Tenure

Substantial rights to a job cannot be acquired just by
accepting a job. Performance in the job setting provides
the index to decision-making. At the time of the initial
contract, teachers are classified as probationary; i. e., they
are on trial. Only upon performance at some minimally
satisfactory quality level can they move toward job security.
Varying from state to state, probation periods are typically
about three years in duration. During that period, evaluations are made which become the basis for a decision about
permanent employment, or the denial of it and "letting the

employee go. " Probation is a period during which the employee is on trial, and sequential and systematic performance
evaluations are made.   The evaluations are discussed with
the employee as suggestions toward performance improvement, and are placed in the employee's personnel file to become matters of record.

Probation is derived from the Latin word which means
"to prove. " In effect, it is the last phase of the selection
procedure.   Varying in length from a few weeks to a year
in typical private sector applications, it is of longer duration
for teachers.   In relatively brief probation periods of, say,
one year, a supervisor might complete formal performance
evaluation reports at the end of the second, fifth, eighth,
and eleventh month. The employee's work record would be
built upon those reports.   The final evaluation report would
typically call for a summarizing recommendation from the
supervisor--for or against permanent employee status.   This
is an obviously crucial time.   Neither the worker nor the
supervisor can treat the probation period perfunctorily if its
values are to be realized.   If the recommendation is favorable, it means that the employee has demonstrated the abilities necessary to perform the job well and should advance
into the category of permanent employee.   For teachers, that
status is generally called tenure. 4

Tenure is a condition of continuing and permanent
employment, conferred upon an employee after successful
completion of the probationary period.   Because it necessarily decreases the flexibility in manpower assignment, and
for other reasons, many public employment administrators
view job tenure as contributory to decreased effectiveness,
because of its rigidity.   Yet permanent employment, tenure,
is a condition protected by statute in many states.   It is
important in any consideration of job security.

Most states have a single teacher tenure law.   For Nebraska teachers, two statutes have been enacted to apply to
the several (six) types of employing school districts.   One
statute is labeled as a tenure law; the other is not.   Substantially, and in effect, the laws are parallel.   Both are
included in Chapter 79 of the Revised Statutes of Nebraska.

79-1254.   The original contract of employment
with an administrator or a teacher and a board of
education of a Class I, II, III, or VI district shall
require the sanction of a majority of the members

of the board. Except for the first two years of
employment under any contract entered into after
February 26, 1975, any contract of employment
between an administrator or a teacher who holds
a certificate which is valid for a term of more
than one year and a Class I, II, III, or VI district shall be deemed renewed and shall remain in
full force and effect until a majority of the members of the board vote on or before May 15 to
amend or to terminate the contract for just cause
at the close of the contract period. The first two
years of the contract shall be a probationary period
during which it may be terminated without just
cause.

The offer and acceptance of a contract for the third year
places teachers in a position of permanent employment, from
which they can be removed only as stipulated in law, and
with due process.

79-1257. Any person who has served or who
shall serve under a contract as a teacher for
three successive school years in a fourth or fifth
class school district, and who begins a fourth year
of service under a contract with such school board
shall thereupon become a permanent teacher unless,
by a majority vote of the school board, the time
be extended one or two years before such teacher
becomes a permanent teacher.

As mentioned earlier, the statutes vary on specifics, but not
in effect. Teacher tenure in some statutory form has been
a goal toward which teachers have driven with hardly any
interruption over the past several decades. All tenure laws
provide for dismissal of incompetent or insubordinate employees, but only after the exercise of due process.

Critical to the passage from probation to tenure are
the performance evaluation records. They are the "grist
for the mill," should a due process hearing occur as dismissal of an employee is considered. There is a substantial literature on supervision and evaluation in schools. Com-
passion must be part of performance evaluation by a supervisor, but, more important to both teacher and administrator
in terms of possible use in a hearing, the evaluation must
be systematic, recognizing up-to-date advances in industrial
psychology, and cognizant of legal obligations. With teacher

accountability increasingly expected in the immediate future, it is reasonable that participation in the development of the personnel evaluation system will be a teacher demand at bargaining time.

Seniority

Seniority is an indicator of rights to the job, as employees are compared within their own group. Length of continuous service is the usual indicator of seniority. Factors which may modify seniority as the single indicator of job assignment suitability include job efficiency, physical stamina, and off-the-job experience. For teachers, the most commonly impinging factor is off-the-job experiences; i. e., teaching experience in some other setting or location.

The most prevalent promotion system is that which is based on seniority. Many governmental agencies, as well as quite a few industrial concerns, would protest that seniority is used for promotion only in the lower grades that are subject to collective bargaining, but the facts are otherwise. The job classification and salary advancement plan often dictates a rigid movement of employees toward seniority. Compared to other public agencies, schools provide minimal latitude for promotions in a single job category, and time requirements result in an organizational lockstep in which teachers with the greatest potential move up no faster than those who are less qualified but are of the same age and length of service. [5]

When a layoff is necessary, who will go? When business picks up, who will be recalled first? When a vacancy occurs, who will fill it? The answers affect the attitudes of people toward their own board or council, toward management, and even toward the operation of the organization. The search for the answers has produced a wide variety of policies. These range from the kind of rugged individualism that puts great emphasis on merit and organizational stability, to the other extreme in which nothing but length of service is considered. Typically, public schools and their teachers tend toward the latter category.

Job security and seniority are not synonymous, although they are obviously related. Seniority approximates job security as long as the jobs themselves exist. In a time of severe cutback, a ten-year employee may have no more sense of security than one with two or three years service. Despite such practical reservations, a seniority system is still viewed by most employees as a step in the direction of security.

Job security is vital to all persons whose existence depends upon steady employment. (And, as has been pointed out, most Americans are in that state of dependence.) Therefore, basic policy statements on how seniority and ability will be weighed can remove some of the employee's uncertainties about the future in the job. Policies address two fundamental worker uncertainties:

1. How secure is my job?
2. Do I know in advance how my school district will allocate jobs?

Clearly stated seniority policies should contribute to that higher morale upon which maximum individual efficiency is so dependent.

On the other hand, grievances can be expected when decisions are made regarding promotions, transfers, and demotions, especially if both ability and seniority are criteria. The introduction of a subjective criterion (ability) is an indicator to management that it needs to be prepared to defend and justify its decision with documentary evidence, such as production records, attendance records, and discipline records. [6] The personnel file, built upon the supervisor's systematic evaluations, must be the source of such evidence.

Labor contracts contain a variety of provisions in which seniority is designated as a deciding factor in times of controversy. In the most extreme case, seniority only is mentioned. Other contracts may say that seniority governs, provided that the senior employee is minimally capable of doing the work. Still others may say that seniority shall be the deciding factor where ability is equal. This places the burden of proof on management, and experience indicates management's heavy dependence upon seniority. This may be due to expediency, the belief that adherence to seniority will foster labor peace, a lack of adequate criteria of ability, or the feeling that the existing evidence of merit differences would not convince an arbitrator should the union file a grievance. In any event, there is a strong tendency for seniority to govern, if it is mentioned at all in the labor agreement. [7]

School boards and other public employers have found, for a number of reasons, that the use of seniority measures is beneficial for them as well as for the employees. Seniority is simple to understand, easy to administer in many ways, and usually has substantial worker support for implementation.

Teachers need to understand several specific questions about seniority. They should be addressed in statute, or in the contract. A sampler of such questions include the following:

1. Does seniority begin at the point of initial hiring?

2. Does seniority begin when probation ends?

3. Is extended absence due to illness excluded from the calculation of seniority?

4. Is time spent on military duty part of the calculation of seniority?

5. Will seniority be the major factor in determining promotions, demotions, transfers, and so on?

6. In cases of equal seniority, how are decisions made?

7. Must the seniority list be publicly posted, periodically?

Many questions must be raised as the implementation of seniority is considered. Some contracts have spoken to the manner in which time may be counted toward seniority. Some samples follow.

Seniority means uninterrupted employment with the University beginning with the latest date of hiring with the University and shall include periods of University employment outside the bargaining unit, layoffs and other periods of absence authorized by and consistent with this agreement. (University of Michigan and AFSCME, exp. 12-73)

The time at which seniority starts is important.

During the probationary period, employees shall

> have no seniority status and may be laid off or
> terminated in the sole discretion of the employer
> without regard to their relative length of service.
> At the conclusion of an employer's probationary
> period, the name shall be added to the seniority
> list as of his last hiring date. (Western Michigan
> University and AFSCME, exp. 7/74)

Seniority lists are, typically, the responsibility of the employer, and many contracts provide for their publicity, and
delineate procedures through which questions may be addressed to their accuracy.

> The employer will maintain an up-to-date unit-
> wide seniority list, a copy of which shall be posted
> on the appropriate bulletin boards and given to the
> president of the union at six-month intervals follow-
> ing the initial posting. The names of all employees
> who have completed their probationary periods shall
> be listed on the seniority list in order of their last
> hiring dates, starting with the employee with the
> greatest amount of seniority at the top of the list.
> (Western Michigan University and AFSCME, exp.
> 7/74)

Seniority is used as a control factor in times of layoff.

> Layoffs shall take place only when there is a
> general reduction in the work force, and then shall
> be based on qualifications and seniority. When any
> members of the bargaining unit who work under the
> aegis of Civil Service must be dropped from em-
> ployment in reverse order of their seniority, they
> shall be placed on a special re-employment list,
> and they shall be re-employed in direct order of
> seniority. (Board of Education, Newark, N. J.,
> and American Federation of Teachers, exp. 1/76)

Seniority provisions, covering many aspects of that condition,
are considered to be among the most important provisions in
any collective bargaining agreement. [8]

In labor relations, seniority came to the fore as a
determinant of many questions about hiring and firing. But
in the context of contemporary concern to improve the job
position of females and non-whites, problems have developed.
In a blanket application of the "last hired, first fired" rule,

the burden of discharge may fall unequally upon females and non-whites, because they have been heavily recruited and hired only recently. Shall strict application of seniority prevail? The answer is not clear and unequivocal, but in McDonald v. Santa Fe Trail Transportation Co. (1976), the Supreme Court ruled on the topic of differentiated application of discipline by race. In this case, McDonald and Laird, the white male plaintiffs, claimed that they had been fired for misappropriating property while a black employee similarly charged was not dismissed. McDonald sought relief under his union's contract, and from the EEOC. Unsuccessful there, he carried the dismissal into civil courts. The Court construed Title VII as protection for whites and blacks alike. It quoted the EEOC, in which was stipulated its congressional "... mandate to eliminate all practices which operate to disadvantage the employment of any group protected by Title VII, including Caucasians"; noted that both the union and employer had discriminated against McDonald; and ruled that protection from discriminatory action was available to all, equally. (This would seem to supersede some district court decisions during the early seventies in which males with seniority were ordered "bumped" at times of layoff, providing work spaces for blacks and females who had been hired under equal opportunity programs.)

Reduction in Force

Reduction in force (RIF) has been defined as

> ... to reduce, cut, trim down to size; often used as a verb, as in, 'Falling enrollments and rising costs forced the school board to RIF half the staff.' Slang: bust, pinkslip, fire. Antonyms: increase, expand, promote, elevate. [9]

RIF is a relatively new addition to the vocabulary of teachers, having been used most especially in the 1970s. The term, more commonly associated with layoff in labor terms, refers to a cutback of jobs for teachers.

In the 1960s, who would have predicted a layoff of teachers? After the great growth of education following World War II, who would have thought that there would be a need to cut back on school staffs in the seventies? However, reduced enrollment, financial exigencies, inflation, low faculty turnover, and changes in student course and program preferences are influencing education, and are forcing boards and teachers to reckon with RIF. RIF does not include dismissal for disciplinary reasons.

Although teacher tenure provides job security, most statutes stipulate that teachers may be dismissed when programs are curtailed, enrollments decline, or for financial exigency, generally. Schools do not exist to provide jobs for teachers. Students must be registered, pursuing programs in which teachers offer courses. Tenure laws do not address the issue of importance to teachers, which is, if layoffs are to occur, in what order will teachers be affected, and what will be the order of recall?

Teachers may be "riffed" only under specific circumstances, when their positions are eliminated as a result of one of the following circumstances:

1. A substantial reduction in the funds available to the Board, provided that such reduction cannot be avoided by the exercise of the Board's taxing or other fiscal powers;

2. a substantial reduction in pupil enrollment;

3. the discontinuance of a particular type of teaching service, provided that such discontinuance is not for arbitrary or discriminatory reasons; or

4. a bona fide consolidation of the school with one or more other school districts. [10]

The conditions under which reduction in force has come to the fore are growing; its likelihood of occurrence is increasing in one after another school district. Schools, more than other social agencies, are likely to need RIF policies or agreements. This is because of the population group which they serve. The following suggestions should be a part of any RIF policy.

1. Do it before you need to do it--a survey conducted in 1973 indicated that scarcely 50 negotiated agreements between teachers and boards named provisions for layoffs of staffs and teachers.

2. Let natural attrition (scheduled retirements, move-aways, nonrenewals of probationary teachers)

of staff have its effect. Then begin "forced attrition" of part-time employees (aides, substitutes and interns, for example) before laying off fulltime substitutes. Make sure all unnecessary items are cut from the budget.

3. Make positions on RIF clear to employees and community members. Explain current enrollments, the financial and employment picture, and tell what experts predict over the next several years.

4. Make sure the district explains why teachers are being laid off.

5. Make sure RIF policies are legal.

6. Consider making RIF a bargainable item at the negotiations table.

7. Set up policies. [11]

During the last ten years, it has been rather typical in school districts that budgets have increased without interruption, that student population has fallen, that faculties and staffs have increased, and that the expenditure per pupil has doubled or tripled. As political units, schools are susceptible of action originating in taxpayer discontent, and incidences of nonsupport are not so uncommon now. Speaking to the political realities, and incorporating most of the seven suggestions above, the Bellevue, NE, Board of Education adopted the following policy in June, 1976:

Reductions in certificated staff which may be required due to decreasing enrollments, limited financial support, changing programs or other factors, will be accomplished, when possible, through the normal procedures of resignations, retirement, leaves of absence and other methods of attrition of staff.

In the event that it becomes apparent that the necessary staff reductions may not be accomplished through the normal attrition of staff, the Superintendent will recommend to the Board of Education the names of those individuals to be terminated under the reduction in force provisions of the continuing contract law.

The selection of personnel for termination shall be done in the inverse order of their length of uninterrupted service with the district, certification and endorsement which may be required to (1) and (2) maintain accreditation, (3) state and federal regulations which may mandate certain employment practices and (4) special qualifications that may require specific training and/or experience. In the absence of the above considerations, length of uninterrupted service shall be the sole determining factor.

Those employees who have been terminated through a reduction in force shall be offered re-employment with the district for a period of two years following the date of termination when vacancies occur for which they are qualified. At re-employment, the employee shall resume the position on the salary schedule or range that is dictated by his/her experience and training, except that the length of time represented by the break in service shall not be included as service with the district.

Administrative regulations implementing the above policy statements shall be developed by the Superintendent of Schools.

Schools without a RIF policy need one. It must be in place ahead of the event. It may be developed unilaterally, as board policy, or carried out at time of negotiations, with equal input from both teachers and administrators. It must allow for systematic application. A checklist of actions for administrators, articulated into a timeline, provides some stability in a situation which is necessarily shocking for the workers affected by RIF. 12

Dismissal, Just Cause and Due Process

Job security has come to public employees as a result of the gradual accrual of one after another safeguard from arbitrary dismissal or discharge. In the pulling and tugging which has occurred when administration, anxious to preserve certain rights of personnel management, has encountered labor, equally anxious to develop protection for workers, many compromises have been developed. These settlements have found their way into contracts and also, through the political clout of unions, into statutes. Dismissal can be only for cause or just cause. This is true for all permanent employees of schools, and often for probationary professional employees as well.

Selections from the Revised Statutes of Nebraska provide an interesting comparison of the statutory stipulations which govern the firefighter-city council relationship, and the teacher-school board relationship when either category of public employee is being considered for dismissal.

14-704. All members or appointees of the fire department shall be subject to removal by the city council under such rules and regulations as may be adopted, and whenever the council shall consider and declare such removal necessary for the proper management or discipline, or for the more effective working or service of the fire department. Before a fireman can be discharged, charges must be filed against him before the council and a hearing had thereon, and an opportunity given such member by his superiors in case of misconduct or neglect of duty or disobedience to orders. Whenever any such suspension is made, charges shall be at once filed before the council by the person ordering such suspension, and a trial had thereon. The council shall have the power to enforce the attendance of witnesses and the production of books and papers, and to administer oaths.

79-1254. The secretary of the board shall, not later than April 15, notify each administrator or teacher in writing of any conditions of unsatisfactory performance or other conditions because of a reduction in staff members or change of leave of absence policies of the board of education which the board considers may be just cause to either terminate or amend the contract for the ensuing school year. Any teacher or administrator so notified shall have the right to file within five days of receipt of such notice a written request with the board of education for a hearing before the board. Upon receipt of such request the board shall order the hearing to be held within ten days, and shall give written notice of the time and place of the hearing to the teacher or administrator. At the hearing evidence shall be presented in support of the reasons given for considering termination or amendment of the contract, and the teacher or administrator shall be permitted to produce evidence relating thereto. The board shall render the decision to amend or terminate a contract based on the evidence produced at the hearing. As used in this section and section 79-1254.02, the term just cause shall mean incompetency, neglect of duty, unprofessional conduct, insubordination, immorality, physical or mental incapacity, other conduct which interferes substantially with the continued performance of duties or a change in circumstances necessitating a reduction in the number of administrators or teachers to be employed by the board of education.

Developed expressly to serve two different public employment settings in a single state, the statutes are conceptually parallel. That is, a permanent employee is statutorily entitled to a hearing before dismissal; in each case, the employing board or council assumes another role, the role of unbiased hearing tribunal. There are two major differences in the statutes:

1. For firefighters, a hearing is mandatory, while for teachers it is optional, if elected by the teacher during the specified period of time.

2. Just cause for dismissal is detailed for teachers, but is left general and open for firefighters.

From this selection of statutes and brief analysis, it is apparent that the content of a public employee contract within a specific state will not be the same for different employee categories. Each occupational category has some unique aspects deserving of contractual treatment.

Cause or just cause is a part of most contracts, in clauses treating of dismissal or discharge. A 1969 survey conducted by the Bureau of National Affairs involved 400 contracts. That study revealed that 82 per cent of the contracts contained a general statement about grounds for dismissal, such as just cause. [13] Dismissal or discharge is so drastic, so final, that the evidence upon which that decision is made must be very persuasive, very strong.

Whether in the contract or statute, questions about

just cause have arisen at the point of application. What does it mean, really? Daugherty developed a succinct yet comprehensive set of seven criteria as standards supporting just cause. The set has had wide acceptance in the public employment sector. In cases of dismissal, all seven questions should be answered affirmatively by the employing board or council.

1. Did the employee have foreknowledge that his conduct would be subject to discipline, including possible discharge?

2. Was the rule he violated reasonably related to the safe, efficient, and orderly operation of the agency's business?

3. Did the agency make a reasonable effort before disciplining him to discover whether he in fact did violate this rule?

4. Was its investigation fair and objective?

5. Did it obtain substantial evidence that the employee was guilty of the offense with which he was charged?

6. Was its decision nondiscriminatory?

7. Was the degree of discipline given him reasonably related to the seriousness of his proven offens and/or to his record with the agency?[14]

Hand in glove with just cause is due process. For consideration and for theoretical analysis, the two may be separated; not so in practice. Because of the reserved authority of management, to separate just cause from due process would be to substantially destroy those techniques as protection for employees. In the United Steelworkers of America v. Warrior & Gulf Navigation (1960), a case alluded to earlier in another context, the Supreme Court stated:

Collective bargaining agreements regulate or restrict the exercise of management functions; they do not oust management from the performance of them. Management hires and fires, pays and promotes, supervises and plans. All these are part of its functions, and absent a collective bargaining agreement, it may be exercised freely except as limited by published law and by the willingness of employees to work under the particular unilaterally imposed conditions.

Due process insists that there should be a reasonable inquiry or investigation into the charges which, when brought against an employee, could lead to dismissal from work. For example, those obligations were clearly stipulated in the Nebraska statutes above. The investigation must be fair and unbiased, not aimed at sustaining the maximum discipline against the employee, i. e., discharge. The burden of proof rests upon management. In settings such as prescribed by the Nebraska statutes--and something comparable would commonly be found in other states--management must abide by the procedural requirements, moving step by step. If, for some reason, an employing board or council should choose to ignore stipulated rules of procedure and to advance, making a decision to discharge the employee in question, that decision would be vulnerable. Even in those situations which appear to be clear-cut, when employee violations are known, the employee is still entitled to whatever due process is specified in the statute or contract. Although some employees may forego the procedure at their option, and accept dismissal from work because they know that the evidence is overwhelming, that choice is for the employee, not for the employer.

When dismissed from work, an employee faces substantial losses. Wages or salary are lost, and American workers, private or public, are dependent upon a steady cash flow as a consequence of their comparatively high rate of consumption. The worker also loses fringe benefits--life and medical insurance, pension benefits, and so on. Additionally, the employee loses seniority, which may not have immediate money value but which obviously has very high value in an extension over the years of the work career. Because job security is precious to the individual, it is, of itself, a contributor to social stability, and Americans have invented techniques and obligations intended to assure that when jobs are lost, they are lost only for bona fide cause, established through due process. All public employees not "covered" by statute should be "covered" by their negotiated contract; contracts may go beyond the "minima" of statute, when it is mutually agreeable to do so. It is in the employee's interest. Less obvious, perhaps, it is also to the interest of individuals who serve on public boards, for it is a protection against suits for liability.

References

1. Fisher, Robert. "When Workers are Discharged--An Overview, " Monthly Labor Review, June, 1973, p. 4.

2. Government Employee Relations Report, 7-11-77, pp. 716:15-17.

3. Bell, Daniel. The Cultural Contradictions of Capitalism. New York: Basic Books, Inc., 1976, pp. 234-35.

4. Lopez, Felix M. Evaluating Employee Performance. Chicago: Public Personnel Association, 1968, pp. 92-93.

5. Ibid., pp. 102-103.

6. Black, James Menzies. The Basics of Supervisory Management. New York: McGraw-Hill, Inc., 1975, p. 139.

7. Miner, John B. and Mary G. Miner. Personnel and Industrial Relations--A Managerial Approach. New York: Macmillan Company, 1973, pp. 237-238.

8. Government Employee Relations Report, 8019-74, pp. 85:2711-2761.

9. Nolte, Chester M. "Follow These 'How-To's' When You Must Cut Your Staff." The American School Board Journal, July, 1976, p. 23.

10. Wollett, Donald and Robert Chanin. The Law and Practice of Teacher Negotiations. Washington: Bureau of National Affairs, 1974, p. 3:71.

11. Nolpe, op. cit., p. 27, 45.

12. Mumford, Peter. Redundancy and Security of Employment. Guildord, Surrey England: The Gower Press, 1976, pp. 147-150.

13. Baer, Walter E. Discipline and Discharge Under the Labor Agreement. New York: American Management Association, 1972, p. 3.

14. Ibid., p. 29.

Chapter 10

EPILOGUE

Labor relations in American public employment in the past were essentially a matter of cooperation, as large but relatively weak employee organizations accepted work conditions which were established unilaterally by the employing boards and councils. This was especially true for teachers. Viewed from the latter seventies, those conditions now appear as simple work settings, simply administered in government agencies which had uncomplicated missions and goals. With militant unions now on the scene, and with many new obligations and restrictions mandated for public service agencies, public employment is no longer a simple work structure. In the sense that it is composed of labor and management, advocates for both "sides" in this new structure add but little to the store of knowledge through which both employee productivity and compensation can be improved. Advocates have a tendency toward intractable positions, from which they only add fuel to a raging debate, and provide very little real illumination.

Despite all the problems to which teachers, administrators and public school trustees may be so sensitive, despite the recriminations which do occur, and the strikes which have halted the educational enterprise on occasion, perspectives need to be lengthened. To view the whole enterprise in the heat of present conflicts is to assume a short-range, debilitating position. There is need to note where we were, to recognize our present problems and opportunities, and to establish our expectations and hopes for the future.

There were times when applicants for positions as teachers were selected with preference given to one sex or the other; to people who were married, or sometimes to the unmarried. Direct relationships between applicant qualifica-

176

tions and job performance were not always clear. Teachers taught under contracts in which many minute details of their personal lives were stipulated. Among all public employees, teachers had perhaps the most restrictions put upon them, partially because of their role-model function. The compensation was comparatively poor, and it was not all uncommon for teachers to be paid in no-fund warrants which, if they could be exchanged at some local bank, were always cashed at a discount.

Very few of those early twentieth-century conditions still prevail. Teachers have about as much freedom in their personal lives as other citizens do. If teacher salary increases have not out-distanced those of public employees in other occupations, data indicate that they have at least kept pace. Fringe benefits, including teacher tenure, compare very favorably with the private sector. But the public is concerned about school productivity. Paying scant attention to the student body which changed radically during the 1960s, questions about the lower scores on nationally administered tests by public school graduates--as evidence of less learning--are coming to the fore. Teachers have been successful in achieving considerable occupational equality with other job categories, and citizens are now saying, "Let them demonstrate their capabilities in high productivity." Surveys show clearly that the public is dissatisfied with the production of the schools.

There are problems and opportunities in the future. Some of them must be addressed by teachers. They are, after all, charged with the responsibility to lead children in learning. Some problems, then, are professional performance problems. If the public becomes convinced that its money, paid in taxes, is supporting malfunctioning schools staffed by teachers who do not care, collective bargaining will not be important. It is only a technique through which compensation levels and other matters are determined. That is, how much pay should be delivered for a valuable service? To the extent that this educational service is perceived by patrons as being done less well than in some previous time--for whatever reasons--teachers have a professional problem which will plague them in bargaining.

With public appreciation of the educational service stabilized, then collective bargaining techniques may be continued and refined. Many employment uncertainties loom in the future as tax bases erode and financing becomes as much a political as an educational consideration. Taking only one area as an example, what is going to happen in equal employment opportunities? How will equal employment, finally, be defined? If quotas or ratios are to be part of it, how will they be determined?

In contract conditions from the past, certain basic responsibilities are apparently so important to schools that they will prevail in the future. They are basic teaching functions, professional obligations which can be evaluated by a supervisor. The following list is typical of such responsibilities:

1. Teachers are responsible for their instructional plans.
2. Teachers must keep and report records of absence and tardiness.
3. Teachers must be aware of their school district's policy.
4. Teachers must follow the curriculum, as specified.
5. Teachers must protect and conserve the property of the school.

Collective bargaining for public employees is not a process which is likely to be reversed. Too many people are interested in its extension for that to happen. Yet the details and specifics are not firm and immutable; they will change.

In America, we embrace the principle that each citizen is free to make a choice of occupation. Many will choose a service occupation and will work in some agency in a political subdivision, such as a public school district. As public sector collective bargaining matures, both labor and management would do well to recall a comment by John Gardner, who said in 1969,

> We have in the tradition of this nation a well-tested framework of values; justice, liberty, equality of opportunity, the worth and dignity of the individual, brotherhood, individual responsibility. These are values that are supremely compatible with social renewal. Our problem is not to find better values but to be faithful to those we profess-- and to make those values live in our institutions.

INDEX OF CASES, BY TOPIC

INDEX

184 / Index